A SHORT HISTORY OF SNAKES

A SHORT HISTORY OF SNAKES

POEMS

ALAN JENKINS

GROVE PRESS
New York

Published simultaneously in Canada
Printed in the United States of America

FIRST EDITION

Library of Congress Cataloging-in-Publication Data

Jenkins, Alan, 1955–
   A short history of snakes : poems / Alan Jenkins.
     p. cm.
   ISBN 0-8021-3811-X
   I. Title.
   PR6060.E517 S46 2001
   821'.914—dc2l   00-069615

Design by Laura Hammond Hough

Grove Press
841 Broadway
New York, NY 10003

01 02 03 04   10 9 8 7 6 5 4 3 2 1

CONTENTS

UNCOLLECTED POEMS

ACKNOWLEDGMENTS

For Melissa, with thanks

PARTY GOING

Just finding the place was an act of love.
Signposts, maps deceived us as we drove
And drove, not speaking, through incessant rain.
The windshield wipers' rhythmic screech
Ran back and forth, hot knife
Behind the eyes, entering a nerve or vein.
Water gushed and splayed from unseen heights
Across far-funneling black, the Downs stepped off
Into nothing, where a few smudged lights shone;
A blurred loom became two headlights
That bored steadily through us and were gone.
For hours, we traced the same roads over fields,
Each track returning with the sense of shapes,
Known, familiar—hedges, trees, massed hills—half-
Defined, the negative of landscapes.

It seemed we might have driven round all night,
And then forever—locked into a tight
And tightening circle. Miles away,
Tyres bit into gravel, splashed through mud
In cart tracks leading to the oast house.
Inside, rooms were fired to a circular blaze,
Painted masks bobbed out of shadow where
Little smoky groups crouched on rug-strewn floors.
A pale green face twitched uncontrollably.
Incense and marijuana mixed a pungent air
That thickened round figures you could hardly see,
And the walls had turned the color of blood
By the time we arrived . . . Or was it
All dreamt up while we tried to drowse
In the middle of a field, dead drunk, unfit

To go on or back? Of morning, all I remember is
The tangled thicket, briars and blackberries
Like smoking entrails, the dark, delicate
Clusters of blood clots, drenched,
And the hedges' crown of thorns
Draped with mist, grey half-light, the quiet;
The long grass under nets of frost;
Then the distant, sudden blare of horns
As if something had been accomplished,
The knowledge coming back that we were lost.
Whatever it was then that I wished,
Some loosening, like a fist unclenched,
Some final warmth—I felt a spreading ache
Through both my arms, and found two burns
Such as a rushlight or a brand would make.

(1976: Sussex)

FROM
IN THE HOTHOUSE

IN THE HOTHOUSE

Tropical fir trees, tendril trails
of liana,
locked in together, have their fun.

A cathedral that's wet and warm!
Loudspeakers fill our ears
with the shrieking of children and birds,

a steady murmuring of prayer.
There's a nasty storm
but it's still paradise. The kind of air

you'd expect to find in Guiana,
the drenched fronds
of palm and fern, a thousand of our closest friends.

The Grand Duke's window. Poisonous snails.
Boxwood sleeping in the sun.
The hose pipe's coils. You're lost for words.

THE OLD TUNE

I was walking past a patch of waste ground
that doubled as front lawn and battlefield
for a block of council flats—
windows boarded, everything and everybody running riot—
when I heard them drifting from high up,
climbing higher, the clear notes
of a single phrase
played on an alto saxophone.
The sound made its own kind of quiet—
that rich pause before each stop.

These were the dog days,
this was August, English summer heat-wave heat.
The music knocked me off my feet
and blew my head away
to Paris, 1970:
a boy of fifteen
on my own for the first time in that city,
I'd been driven up and down the *quais*
by a student not much older than myself
I'd befriended on the Dunkirk train.

He fixed me up in a hotel
on one of the smarter streets in Passy.
The ironwork of the lift, the view of the Tour Eiffel
were nothing to what I saw and heard
one night, getting into bed—
from across the courtyard
came a tune played on the sax,
so sweet . . .
And in the window, a man's silhouette,
a girl swaying close, tuning up for sex.

I listened as it all went down.
I watched her giving head.
I carried that tune like a talisman.
And I've heard saxophonists since then
who've opened the world up wider
than Marlon Brando
Maria Schneider,
wider than the eyes of that girl in the window,
than even Belmondo
murmuring to no one *Marianne, Marianne.*

TEETH

We ended up as we'd begun:
sitting on a bed in someone's house,
a party going on downstairs, between us
every kind of trouble—
the first time, we'd gone against the grain
of the stripped-pine kitchen, our hosts' ifs and buts,
and were bent double
trying to get in touch. Our mouths wouldn't fit
on account of your two front teeth.
Every muscle felt the strain.
We finished in a heap on the floor,
nerve ends holding out for more . . .
Then shared the mattress with another couple.
That night we were almost undone—
a pinprick would have burst the bubble—
but all we exchanged were love bites.

Now here we were again,
two different people
in another stranger's bedroom,
doing something . . . illicit.
I was like Miss Lonelyhearts,
dejected, down-at-heel, plucking at your nipple
with finger and thumb,
lifting the shirt off your back,
taking a free hand to your gusset . . .
This time what we did was nothing new—
until, that is, you said, "I only want
to hurt you, now," took me between your teeth
and bit. I couldn't see much point
in staying around to talk,
though I could see something in your point of view.
I took a deep breath and said, "It hurts."

your telephone blaring, off the hook,
a drunken voice on the intercom,

a round spy hole of light
in the steamed-up window.

The pacing of your neighbor
who is haunted, even now,

by the fact that he mistook
your final, bloodcurdling scream

for the noise you often make
when he urges you to come. . . .

You wake
in a tangle of sheets,

reach for the familiar, hard
flesh beside your own—

something is there
(though you cannot feel a single bone),

curled around its head,
scaly, rustling, wet.

Without a word,
he slithers out of bed

and down the stone
stairs, stops to light a cigarette.

MARILYN AND YOU

From one of her sky-high heels, Marilyn
would lop off
a quarter of an inch,
a horseshoe in miniature,
so that she could toe the line
the more unsteadily
between insanity and lunch,
or walk a high-tension wire
she could never see the end of
(they always gave her too much or too little rope);
she went skeetering, all ass-wiggles,
hip-swayings, thigh-jiggles,
down a shocking slope
to the bed where they found her jackknifed.

Photographs would have her looking well dressed
in black high heels
and not much else.

You wear yours to parties—that little lift—
and look unsteady only when you're drunk, or bored
off-balance.
You've never used them to pin any part of a man
to the floor, or stamp a military tattoo
on his chest.
I've seen them flung anyhow in the cupboard
among the bras and pants
and given them a second glance.
I've watched you, after half a mile, totter
and almost fall. Go barefoot rather than.

FEAST

At a table in a fisherman's house in Sète
the fisherman's son and ten or twelve of us, his friends—
French and English, the Algerian girl—all sat
and opened oysters with our bare hands,

oysters from a barrel that was sprigged with seaweed,
bottomless, as though he had sunk a well
to a saltwater lake below the house, an oyster bed.
I plunged in for another crusted shell

and it released the reek of seaweed and sea, reek of a girl.
The barrel stood as high as our chests
and the plates were stacked with mother-of-pearl.
I watched the black points of Khedidja's breasts

jiggling inside her shirt, and flushed with *apéros*
and *vin rosé,* I wanted to still them, so thought I'd try
to sit her on my lap like a powdered fop from Paris
in *Le déjeuner d'huîtres* by Jean François de Troy.

OR WOULD YOU
RATHER NOT BE SAVED

That night I turned up at her place soon after nine—
the friend of a friend, I had the usual contacts—
two girls were waiting. That was the first surprise.
The next came after some chaste chat of this and that
when the conversation took a turn for the worse
and the way they handled the vodka martinis
left me reeling, trying to explain
a morning glory. They'd never heard. They laughed
as I trotted out the half-remembered facts,
the bladder filling, the all-important nerve,
the pressure, the inevitable rise.
Another drink? Sure, why not. I talked with verve
and a handful of nicely balanced ironies
about the flattery such simple unconscious acts
as turning to someone, on waking, could imply—
I was telling this against myself, of course,
for how else should they interpret my sudden shaft
of half-feigned bitterness? And that was why,
when I sank back and saw both pairs of eyes on mine,
the eyes and the air between us seemed alive
with expectancy, or hope. A light acid rain
fell on the windows, the ticking of clocks
filled a split second's silence, and the hive
in my head buzzed with the usual swarm
of memories, dreamlike adrenalin-administered shocks
at the forms desire can take, when it takes form.

Were we going out? We were. A moment later
we hit the street. The pavement was a sidewalk,
not a pavement, so I knew we were in New York.
It struck me that rather than use my given name

they both referred to me as Mickey Finn.
They seemed to find that amusing. *Would it be McCool?*
I settled for *You can call me Al.* It sounded lame.
We reached a bar, all three of us (the friend
seemed to be along for the ride). Both were pretty,
one of them, dark and sloe-eyed, hardly spoke
while the other, blond, aggressive, witty,
turned everything, herself included, into a joke.
I was already in two minds, so sat down
between them, and after a while—if I'd dared to look
it would have been as obvious as an open book—
a slim hand came to rest tattoo-lightly on each thigh.
And stayed there. Something stirred. I was trying to focus
on a tiny earring that winked and flashed from a waiter
(and, at the same time, to catch the barman's eye
for two fresh margaritas) when the floor
came up to meet me, the ceiling went into a spin
and the walls began to fly apart.
They helped me to my feet. I tottered. *Crazy
limey sons-of-bitches, lousy motherfuckers*
was the judgment muttered by the barman
backed up by something that was half grimace, half frown
as I staggered off and through a swinging door
leaving him to entertain Dolores, nickname Carmen,
and Faye, also known, apparently, as Daisy,
with his tale of how a guy named *Lionel . . . Lionel . . .
Johnson, from New Jersey, someplace like that . . .*
had died by falling from that same high stool.
A hat? Oh sure, he always wore a hat.
I swayed down a corridor I thought would never end
and into a rose garden I'd never hoped to enter—
music flowed out from a fountain in the center
like water from a rock—"Drugs, alcohol, little sister"—
and at every turn I stumbled on a vista
that for elegance outdid Versailles or Vaux;
a bowery chamber wherein at last I sate
gave on Niagara Falls, the Empire State,

and the Golden Gate Bridge, San Francisco.
It was there I almost left my heart.

In fact I just managed to keep it to myself
and by the time I staggered out, having said good-bye
to the drinks, the taco chips, an olive or two,
the fountain had gone, the roses also, and the only view
was of a tiled wall, a mirror, some basins and a shelf
that ran along it. I loosened my tie,
dipped and cupped my hands, brought them to my face
as though these were the last drops of water on earth.
Straightening up, I looked myself straight in the eye—
or meant to, for what I saw in its place,
rising from the depths of the glass, was this:
the familiar eyes, the pink-rimmed smile, a trace
of cruelty in the lines of the mouth, blowing me a kiss
and beckoning me down a passage lit like a tomb
that I might have seen before. The lips moved
and I heard these words: *I see your health's improved.*
Listen now to what I say, for what it's worth.
You know I've made the chandeliers in this room
shake with laughter, and looked long and deep
in this huge mirror down one wall. You know
already what's been done to me, and by whom,
on this carpet or that bed,
and once upon a time, at this table, I spread
two crooked lines, one of heroin, one cocaine.
All that's over and done with now.
The numbers in my book, the shrill prr-prr
from the telephone, are useless as the row
of party dresses you often flicked through,
the miniature Manhattan on the shelf,
the books and records thrown on one collapsing heap,
the shoes and nylons spilling from a drawer.
Do you still think of me, of what we were?
One day I'll wake up on a cold bare floor,
past all pain, feeling not quite myself.

The lips faded like a faintly glowing ember
and others now appeared where they had been.
They tried to work themselves into a smile
then writhed and spat. *I'm the party queen*
of avant-garde New York, and London too. Remember?
You ought to. You looked me up in my hotel,
took me to dinner, and I made it worth your while.
I guess you could call this my season in hell.
That's Ram-bo. You know, like Rambo Reagan.
An evil enchanter of the world. I'm stoned again.
But it's not my fault. First they'd spike my drink,
and then spike me. I've felt so many pairs of hands
getting in on the act, and after so many one-night stands
I've come round, vaguely, to the beast with two backs,
or woken from a nightmare to its stink.
Even when I slept two to a room,
chatelaine of my elect society,
I couldn't keep out a third, pushy member.
He wore suspenders, fishnet stockings and mascara
and must have known my reputation for sobriety.
The noise he made all night, trying to come,
woke my roommate—getting used to the dark
she stared, fascinated, at my hurry
to fan, with my own hand, a live spark
from that dead or dying ember.

I was beginning to wonder what kind of club
I was in—it would have been known to Groucho Marx,
that much was certain—when this face, too,
dimmed slowly and went out. All I'd heard
had materialized before me, every word—
on the mirror, in a lipstick scrawl.
I was about to go through it once again
when there swam lazily into my ken
these brown-baked features—a corpse, almost,
so tightly were they drawn, or an actual ghost—
that seemed to have burnt up from within,

a map of torments printed on the skin.
I thought I knew him, but all the same shrank back.
I was a writer once, he said, a bit like you.
(I could have said he taught me all I knew.)
I suppose I looked for inspiration in the sack—
or myself. But this is no time for small talk.
You'll want to know how I got to be this way
and how the writing comes to be on the wall.
Maybe when you've heard what I have to say
you'll make a note of it. There have always been messages
scribbled, in the morning, in lipstick, on mirrors.
That time, it was the usual comedy of errors—
the pickup (he looked snug in his denims, streetwise),
the cocktails, the poppers, a shower and massage,
the two-hour acrobatics—man, that boy could fuck—
the pillow talk and sleep-drenched eyes.
Right enough, I'd not believed my luck
but when I woke, it seemed my luck had changed:
I reached for him, but while I'd dozed
he'd taken off, my wallet with him, I supposed.
Well, it hadn't. But when I went into the bathroom
I entered a different dream, one that still goes on—
he'd been jacking up, and had opened a vein,
and was slumped, still naked, on the john,
blood everywhere, and on the mirror, his bright red daub
smeared with a finger: WELCOME TO THE AIDS CLUB

With that, a stem of pain shot through him;
he winced, trembled like a heat wave
and faded. Nor did I take my leave
less swiftly. I was shivering like an icy fire,
cold sweat ran off my limbs and torso
as I groped my way out of the door, a-
long the purple passage with upholstered walls
and back towards the restaurant, the barman,
to Faye or Daisy or (had I heard her saying?) Cora,
to Dolores, also known as Carmen.

I thought I'd been gone two hours or so
but no one took much notice—they were higher
than a pair of kites, or two kids still in college—
as I sat down. Someone was singing,
Do you want to go to heaven, or would you rather not be saved?
We all agreed we'd had one too many highballs,
so how about some food? It came. We sat and ate.
Avocado salad. The salmon of knowledge—
the raw and the cooked—on everyone's plate.
A bottle or two of California Chablis.
I must have been carried out on a stretcher
and felt about as popular as Wild Bill Hickok
at the Crazy Horse, or an SS uniform at Rick's.
After that things are a little sketchy
but the yellow cab showed ten dollars on the clock
and there was an odd scent that reminded me
of a trip to Honfleur, Rouen, Nîmes and Nice,
the Ile St. Louis: ten years—all Annie's—
were on the clock, the clock had stopped, the cabbie
looked askance as though to ask what kind of bum
would leave a girl that way, and what a girl,
Second Avenue was running like the Styx
as we poured ourselves inside and back upstairs,
I was murmuring about the rooftops of Paris
in the early morning, alabaster breasts in a wide bed,
a jet-black triangle, dripping, stepping from the shower
and a towel wrapped like a turban round her head
when my companions shrieked *Paris? Is that Paris, Texas?*
Would you be a desert heart? and we had all come
to ourselves in another dimension—theirs.
Someone was making a commotion in the next world
or in the next room down the hall—*A girl needs a gun*
these days on account of all the rattlesnakes—
a joint was in my hand, I talked for an hour
about the yeti, a shy beast, born of rejection,
and drank the bitter coffee that bubbled in the kitchen
until the theme was exhausted, there was nothing left to do

but sink deeper into the scatter-cushions,
watch half-comprehending while they kissed
(I'd never seen so many uses for a tongue, or lips),
whispered and giggled softly—*How like you this?*—
and toyed with each other's earlobes and hair
so that by the time they sidled out, hip to hip,
hands resting gently on each other's shoulders,
I was about two thousand years older,
I was looking for a lost key, an old place, I was there
already, they were seeping from my touch—
it really didn't seem to matter overmuch—
in that dark wide realm where we sleep with everyone.
The next thing after the next thing I knew
the sheet they'd draped over me like an afterthought
was inching its way down my body, taut
with fear, or perhaps it was merely apprehension;
in the waning darkness I could make them out,
standing to left and right, naked, each holding one corner
and holding themselves, with their free hands,
in a state of extreme creative tension;
I tried to move but was held by invisible bands,
by the arms of Mary Jane, Mary Ann or Mary Warner,
by the gaze of Daisy, the glories of Dolores—
as well as mine, that everything now pointed to,
that, it was clear, my short immodest stories
had, in their eyes, fallen far short of;
unable to contain myself, I was on the rack
and pointed my own accusing finger back.
This must be my comeuppance. *Are they for real?*
was just about the only thing I thought of.
To this moment I can't say. I needed rest.
I watched the light come up in the west
over fire escapes, trellises, brick, iron and steel,
the last stars going out; got up and dressed
and walked the five blocks back to my hotel,
my eyes fixed on the tattooed star on Dolores's breast,
on the down that dusted Daisy, her dorsal swoop and swell.

18

CRAB

Above their miniature promontories
the gulls circle, circle,
or swoop
to grow fat on fish heads. Easy pickings . . .

This late sun greys everything—
water, chain-printed mud,
cliff wall and the Harbour View Hotel
are made of one metal.

Down at the rocks
a small boy
picks his way,
ankle-deep in yellowish scud,

then hunkers over
his wobbly reflection in a pool
to look right through it:
weed like girls' hair,

the rust-red blobs
of anemone, cutthroat
cuttlebones, barnacles
like coolies' hats.

He puts a hand
into that clear soup
to lift a pebble,
and sees the crabs

scuttle sideways, carrying their backs.
It is terrible,
how quickly they are gone
in a swirl of water,

a puff of sand.
Starfish, rank urchins,
dried sea things
collect on a shelf

in the kitchen where
a crab is dressed for dinner,
and I stoop
once more, while there's time, to lose myself.

IMAGINE MY
MOTHER DANCING

or stopping in the nursery late at night.
She will appear in pearls and a new fur,
a cloud of perfume and a burst of light
from a diamond hair clip. That's her,
pouring cocktails from a silver shaker
into a glass like an upturned parasol, glancing
at Daddy. Imagine her dancing,
looking over someone's shoulder for a sign
from him—that he's watching her, that he thinks
she's beautiful . . . How her eyes shine,
something to do with all those drinks,
with memory. Stubbing cigarettes in the sand,
pursing her lips for the lipstick/mirror, taking my hand
and drawing me to her suddenly in a crowd
out shopping one afternoon, laughing too loud
at Daddy's jokes. *Imagine my mother dancing.*

SORTING

Back in the room you called your den:
a whiff of gas, of varnish, turps,
old rags and rust. Piles of papers,
letters, cuttings, drawings, then
the box of ribbons, buckles, medals, shells—
sorting them, I'm in your element, remote
from literature, my mummy's-boy self . . .

The German fighter-pilot's leather coat
that always hung behind the door
except on bonfire afternoons—I wore
it through my teens, and loved its smells
of leather and tobacco, its lining flecked
with whisky stains; the collar I turned up
like a '40s hero, laconic and aloof
(ripped seams, ruined patches proof
of my ten years' neglect . . .)

These must be sorted too: the shelf
of green- and orange-covered Penguins, Conrad, Maugham,
Simenon (she still calls upstairs—
Your supper's nearly ready. Mind you keep warm—
and sings "Bali Hai" to the cats). For forty years,
you dreamt of folly like Almayer's.
Foxed pages, bindings disintegrate.
Pipes. Fishing tackle. You were more like Maigret.

TIES

The dark green Tootal with white spots he wore
in the first photograph of him I saw—
the tie he lent to me for my first date

and later told me I could keep,
the matching scarf too. So 1930s,
I might as well have been in the war.

Two autumn-coloured, large-check ties
that gave me, so I thought, the air
of a schoolmaster out of Evelyn Waugh.

Then the red houndstooth, a bracing affair
with a dash of gin-and-it or *Brighton Rock*,
a lounge lizard's whiff of the paddock.

The last, that I've worn once, I took
because I had to: black, a sort of crêpe
he bought for funerals, and hated.

THE PROMISE

Your "just getting hold of a boat
and going off" was always a possibility,
though each year it looked more remote.
They're still there, waiting: the jetty
and an M.F.V., and the inn,
weatherboard and varnish, high stools
ranged along the bar—*The Spanish Main,*
I've seen it—waiting too. Our rooms would have
that smoke and whisky smell, a masculine
perfection. We'd never shave
closer than a quarter-inch of stubble, you'd perform
your favorite role, the Outcast of the Islands,
mad for rum and mescalin.
And the only real ship of fools
would bring them from Miami for the season,
paying to the hilt to chase marlin,
bewildered by our surly silence.
At night we'd be running firearms
to Cuba or Jamaica, lashing down tarpaulin,
taking money for old rope in the Keys—
you'd keep your knack of riding out the storms.

MY FATHER'S WINTERS

Flushed, unfussed, unreluctant, dapper,
you masterminded the bonfire, the Guy, the Catherine wheels.
I came trotting at your gum-booted heels
when you strode up to light the blue touch-paper
and retired, suddenly a silhouette
drawing on the umpteenth cigarette.

Or you'd hang around in your ex-Naval Reserve
duffle coat, one of the boys, diffident, reserved
and smiling, buying rounds from the pub that didn't close
all night, while I stamped and froze
and clutched a hot dog, a cup of soup,
watching the Regent Street lights go up.

It was snow you hated most, and there was snow
the day we burnt you; and a week or so
after, the neighbors had a mass said for you
though you hated all religions too—
snow on the church, the crib, the shepherds and kings,
like a blueprint I found among your things.

The year you retired for good, you got away—
a cottage on an estuary, a friend, some booze.
In the photograph he took of your back
the sky, the mudflats and water are the same dull grey
and you're wearing duffle coat and boots,
looking out, scenting tar, salt, seaweed and wrack.

TALKING TO
THE UNDERTAKER

For N

We went to see a woman with a tarot pack,
a glass globe and a chart of the Zodiac

before we were both semiorphaned.
She took in her own two hands, my hand,

and saw, as if it were a screen—*like
television, honestly*—in one long look

that everything would work out *in the end
between you and your friend,*

plotted my life as if
she'd read it, saw my father coming to grief,

saw *water, sunlight on an estuary,*
a steel-grey sheet *of silk or mercury—*

it was like something given
in trust, the light of every new beginning—

saw an Anglepoise tilted upwards
as if receiving light, a sheet of words . . .

With darkness by six there comes
not the odor of sunless chrysanthemums

but the unmentionable odor of death,
a rasping of breath

and the glare on each white wall
of the burning hospital,

a sheet turned down, a trace
on your mother's porcelain face

of a light more rich
than that to which

Caravaggio abandoned a boy in awe and fear,
more subtle than the light Vermeer

ushered gently through a window in Delft
for the marriage of dust motes, flesh and air.

She said: *The deceased will be myself.*

FROM
GREENHEART

HEAT

So this was the Isle of Pines—halfway
through Co. Kerry . . . The Isle of Pines!
It flares up in the mind
like a match flame, and is gone.

We chafe each other for the hot, wet spark
and now, land masses melting, glaciers melting—
watched by satellite, miles above our heads . . .
Then wake up dead in our beds.

An archaeologist or hunter-gatherer, the first
to emerge from primeval forest
is led by what's left of his nose
to a strangely glittering black barrow:

sheets of polythene held down by row
on row of tyres. Unnatural quiet. Unnatural dark.
Inside, a litter of bones, bottles, tins; a few
cyanide capsules in a box marked SHELTER.

*

A thousand million tiny fish
in a flap, helpless on the sheet—
which one will dare
the path between the barbed-wire fence

and the wall of heat?
(On one side, women stare
at blank eyes. Blank eyes stare back.
A Sad Sack

guard
will whip out his own Cruise
and demonstrate its use.
It is already hard.

Night and day,
a welter of wood smoke, mud; the tents
of sticks and stones and black plastic rubbish
bags; the darkening silos.)

*

I cycled five miles through potato fields and forest,
past the Deer Haven, Canine Country Club
and Lobster Claw. The hub
of the bicycle I'd borrowed

clicked and whined; she was behind, on an older model,
struggling a little. Halfway between the home of Robert Frost
and that of Robert Penn Warren, I walked in through maple
and spruce pine, and, with her beside me, rowed

my son across the moonlit lake. Hers,
by the wide brown eyes. The jagged silhouettes of firs,
the denser mass of mountain peaks. He bent close to tell me
that every river in Vermont was dry—the dripping oar,

his small voice the only sounds; we could see two hayricks
burning, cars in lay-bys burning. I struck out for the shore.
While she and I lay down among the melting rocks
he would water his one bare tree.

SOFA

In a lay-by just outside Southampton, L.I.,
a four-seater beige plush sofa
sat under trees, as if for some shade and a rest,
as if it had put down roots. Who had laid it by?

Heavy petting under the constellations,
her chewing gum swallowed, his hand on her breast,
the radio playing in a parked Studebaker
and the moon silvering a field of rutabaga . . .

Someone had wanted it to suffer
the indignity of exposure—rips and stains
down all its velvet-covered length, its fringe;
bums who stopped to sleep on it (but there are no bums

on Long Island), and pissed themselves, or worse—
and this had been the perfect revenge
on the hated in-laws, whose wedding gift
it was, way back. A casualty of wars

too old and awful for words, the alcohol wars,
wife-wars, the skirmishes of mobile homes,
it had featured in a nightmare of repossession,
had a story to tell, a sad one, of continental drift.

KÉRKIRA

Pinecones on the roof outside the window
and littering the fern-shadowed path,
the smarting from each pinecone
turned to smoke.
                    Dew-drench.
The room like a Turkish bath,
a mildew map on the ceiling, mildew stench.

The scorpion as it scuttles from the stone,
the lizard blinking in its hexagon of sun.

The tattered pages of *Swann's Way*
ranged on the windowsill alongside M. M. Kaye.

The pink neoclassical façade
of the watering place
where sheep and goats may safely graze,
its fresco of lichen, its dripping green shade.

The mirror painted with LOVE
in the psychedelic years. A frazzled wasp.

Olive leaves shimmying to the slightest breeze,
a donkey groaning under its hump of straw.
A moped leaning on a wall of heat.

A jangle of wire nerves behind the door,
the water pipes' asthmatic wheeze,
the clack and rasp
of shutters thrown back on themselves.

A grinning peasant-Prospero calling for Miranda
from the orange or the lemon grove.

Cockroach husks, mosquito ghosts on shelves.
The umpteenth glass. The umpteenth card.

The black bee as big as a clenched fist,
fireflies winking and flashing the way home
to a bare room,
a wide brass bed, a damp white sheet.

Rain in the pine forest. Love-in-a-mist.

RAIN IN THE PINE FOREST
(from D'Annunzio)

Hush. The edge
of the forest. I can't hear
those human words
you're saying,
only the language
of distant
raindrops and leafage.
Listen.
It's raining from the strung-out
clouds. It's raining
on the tamarisks,
salty, parched;
on the scaly,
bristling pines,
on the sacred
myrtle,
on the broom that flames
with clusters of flowers,
on the junipers,
thickly hung
with scented berries,
raining
on our leaf-surrounded faces,
on our bare hands,
our flimsy
clothes, on our two minds,
freshened, still thirsting;
on the beautiful fiction
which yesterday
seduced you, which
today seduces me,
my lover.

Do you hear? The rain falls
on this abandoned
forest growth
with a rustling
that comes and goes,
deepens, fades on the air
as the leaves are more or less
scarce.
Listen. Only
the cicada's song
replies to the sound of weeping, a song
that neither
the murmured lamentation of the south
nor the ashen sky
appals.
And the pine makes one sound,
the myrtle another, the juniper
yet another,
each one an instrument
played by innumerable fingers,
and we
are wholly immersed
in the spirit of the forest,
we are alive with the trees' life,
and your intoxicated features
are rain softened like a leaf,
your hair has the scent
of the glowing broom,
earthly creature
whom
I call
my lover.

Listen, listen. Those airy nothings the cicadas
are drowned out little by little,
but a hoarser song
rises from the remote

dank shadows—
the one note
that trembles, fades,
rises, trembles, fades.
We cannot hear
the sea's voice,
or anything but the splash and hiss
of drenching, purifying, silver rain,
a noise of metal being beaten—
louder, fainter, as
the leaves are more or less
close.
The frog, daughter of the distant marshlands,
is singing from shadowy dark somewhere,
and the rain falls on your eyelashes—
it's as if you wept,
but with pleasure—
as green-white you emerge
like a dryad from the bark.
We twine and part,
twine and part, like thickets,
their greenness fetters and ensnares us,
it's raining on our sylvan faces,
our hands, our flimsy
clothes, our freshened souls,
on the beautiful fiction which yesterday
seduced me, today
seduces you, my lover.

KEEP-NET

We are fishing again, the Thames at Teddington, the two
of us have cycled here to set up canvas stools
on the towpath, and are fishing, some six feet apart,
slightly less than the length of my boyish greenheart rod,
that one day I shall watch disappear into the water
behind a careless canoe, that now bends lightly
as I reel in, and all the past swings lightly
into view, I reel it in, there with the float, the shot,
the shreds of bright green weed, the half-drowned maggot;
I prise the hook out of its mouth and it flashes briefly silver
in the keep-net, but has left a slime of scales on my hand,
there are scenes encoded there, messages I cannot read,
I am a child who mouths Our Father, in my books
Father Thames and Father Time are men with beards, like God;
my father has no beard, but a mustache he once shaved off
and only once, my mother made a fuss till it grew back;
he lights his Imperial Bruyere and it hangs lightly
from his mouth, the bright leaves flicker and I see through
grey-brown water his face coming nearer, bristly, smelling
of pipe smoke; a pile of drawings, a photograph enlarger,
swords and pictures on the walls, a dripping tap;
he runs across the lawn in his dressing gown, maroon
spotted white, and waves his hands to shoo away our cat
that is mauling my ankle, my screams dying into sobs,
his dressing gown billowing; he holds my head above water
as he tries to make me swim. The float bobs, I want him
to catch one too, more than I want to catch them all
myself, I who have caught the past, which is made of him,
maroon or silver flashes in a grey-brown river, into which I
      dive
as my rod, in slow motion, disappears, as the spools
of our reels click and whirr, click and whirr,
the Imperial Bruyere has fallen into my lap
as I wake, a book for keep-net, and mouth *My father.*

LOG

"The maelstrom! Could a more dreadful word in a more dreadful
situation have sounded in our ears! . . . From every point of the
horizon enormous waves were meeting, forming a gulf justly called
'The Navel of the Ocean,' whose power of attraction extends to a
distance of twelve miles. There, not only vessels, but whales are
sacrificed, as well as white bears from the northern regions."
            —Jules Verne, *Twenty Thousand Leagues Under the Sea*

Myself, Fairford and the boy, deckhands on the *Scarface*
(A. G. Pym, Tokyo-Nantucket) were huddled by Buxton, who
        took the wheel,
and Captain George Currie—when Jenkins, gnawing a
        frostbitten sole,
turns to us his fat white mustache of frost and ice,
fluffy-looking, like a kid all stuck with candy-floss
or ice cream from a cornet—but with something of his dad's
who was in whalers before him (*his* dad remembered the days
        of sail).
At first he'd laughed, called it *the rime of the ancient
        mariners,*
but now he turned with a glint in his eye, shouted *Steady lads!*
This here's the maelstrom, the navel of the ocean!
—sort of barmy voice. We thought he'd begun to rave
but looked out, scraping white stars from the ports of the
        deckhouse
and saw, miles around, from every point of the horizon,
running towards the gulf, enormous wave on wave . . .

It was weeks since we'd lost sight of the fleet—seen only pack
        ice
drifting farther and farther south, and not a single whale,
not a single living thing, neither seabird nor seal;
then yesterday, early morning watch, Soutar cried out twice—

Fuckin' Christ man there's bears on it, and peering under the
    fleece
of our hoods we could see them moving, outlines, shadows,
white on whiter white; and terror stabbed each soul
at how long we'd been steaming north. We stood like
    mourners
as Cladd ran for'ard, fired; watched the spirit that was
    Cladd's
explode out of him in a white cloud, a frosty exhalation.
Chedglow chipped him off of the gun with an ice pick;
we boiled and ate most of him, stewed with scurvy cress,
stowed the leftovers, the dainties, which were instantly frozen.
Last night I dreamt of dressed fingers, toes in aspic;

and today we saw the bear we'd skewered—one more
    sacrifice,
crumpled, wasted . . . A moment later we hit the swell,
white swirls, foam plunging, *each wave swallowin' itsel'*,
Soutar screamed, and we were drawn in, down, but not to a
    green-white peace—
for there alongside us, as we sank farther from the floes,
swam a multitude of dead or dying things: otters, gulls, their
    eyelids
clogged shut, fur and feathers claggy with effluents, oil;
among the whaling boats, trawlers, ketches, catamarans
we saw blood-spattered seals, tunny trailing swim bladders;
whales spilling pink froth, each stuck like a huge pincushion
with harpoons; pocked, distended creatures, as from a blasted
    ark—
all this Jenkins begged me to set down, not to secure for us
pardon, still less Larsen's fame, but so that we might keep our
    reason
should we come back alive out of this deep cold, this dark.

PORNOGRAPHY

"Neither cedar of Lebanon,
nor the dome
of St. Paul's,
nor the round heart
of the cemetery, can be seen
from Highgate Hill;
rich Julius Beer
so loathed the world,
would so condemn
his fellow men,
he built here
his huge monument—
thus shutting off
such sights from them
forever. His wife
and womenfolk
consume him forever now
in the public places of hell,
brandish on a fork
his head, and a Bill
of Rights for cannibals."
—Grey, midwinter
light, tangled evergreens;
vaults and sepulchres,
all broken,
crumbling, all overgrown . . .
Silent, we wait
for the sermon on the mount
to continue,
and see—unfurled
among bracken,
holly, ivy, ferns
(wreaths, gone to seed,
flourish on what's inside

the rotting dead),
angels fallen from grace
and shattered urns—
a woman, spread
unnaturally wide,
her flesh stark white
against the black mulch
of earth, of paths
that cover
common graves,
and, black
against it,
thick sprawling thatch;
she leans back
with a full-lipped grin.
You recoil
from the torn
glossy page
and from my thin,
foolish laugh—
you recoil with rage
but she, too, or rather
what was done to her
on this spot
by someone who left
a trail of
cuckoo spit
on the purplish cleft
or across her face—
she, too, as much
as bramble, thorn
and nettle in
impenetrable groves,
is a part of life
in this deathly place . . .
The voice drones on:
our Virgil among

the illustrious
Victorian shades
is open-necked, young,
wears steel-rimmed specs,
has dandruff, a boil,
his mind on sex—
he is telling us
how Dante
Gabriel Rossetti
could not get over
hearing how
his young wife's hair
had gone on growing
in her tomb,
how men saw it glowing
like a glory
by the light
of their bonfire
on the night
they worked to exhume
poems buried with her
as he refused to be—
death-in-life, and art,
and corpse-colonnades
of wealth and fear!

L'ESPRIT D'ESCALIER

*"My room is three and a quarter miles from here, but I must go to
bed as there is a rhinoceros over the mantelpiece."*—Peter Fleming

I had to be picked up and driven down,
of course. In the car three strangers—though not,
naturally enough, to each other—ignored you-know-who
while they recalled weekends in earlier days, a hunt,
a shoot, some legendary do.

It was all hilarious: what Jamie did
when he found them on the billiards table, what Toby said
when Jock jumped ship and nose-dived straight into the quay,
but I couldn't force myself to laugh along with them;
I was a prig, a spoilsport—*me,*

the spare man, mystery guest, backstairs boy.
When I found my dinner jacket laid out on the bed,
my shirt and trousers pressed, I wanted this to happen all the
        time
and wondered if I had *l'esprit d'escalier*
(I thought it meant the wit to climb).

I took an interest in the period and style—
names like *Inigo* and *Capability* began to mean a lot.
How could I say, When I last saw anywhere like this
it was on an outing with my mum and dad—we paid?
Beeches, elms in immemorial stasis . . .

And the rooms! I took a bath in one
that was bigger than my London flat. The maid came in,
fiddled with the sash and was almost out again
before she saw me. I whipped on my flannel fig leaf
and, with a little swish, she was gone.

I'd never given much thought to conversation;
now here I was, simpering for my supper. Was it on
to be the bookish type? No, there was always someone else
who'd read more than I had, who'd published, in fact,
three "really rather good" novels.

I lacked agility *and* confidence—*bons mots*
were beyond me, I never knew who was being talked about.
That left the lovable bohemian, a reprobate, a rake,
charming, ingénue (I once rose when the women did);
definitely gifted; on the make.

Why did the daughters always want it from behind—
was it the childhoods of dogs and horses? Why did they say
Fuck me, harder, oh God, fuck me when I came, as if on cue?
One slipped back to one's room at dawn, before Maisie
        arrived
with tea. But Maisie always knew . . .

I had to be driven back. The morning walks,
the games of patience or charades, the old girls and boys
with beautiful manners; the room where Evelyn Waugh
started *Scoop*. The chapel where I prayed for the patience
to love. To stop being a bore.

PLAYER'S NAVY

Brushing varnish onto brand-new window frames,
sanding edges when the soiled, soaked rag
snags on splinters, I smell the shavings, bright wood
and shining decks of twelve, thirteen; my head swims
with varnish, white spirit, timber smells,
the oil of winches and of oiled wire rope. I tell myself
that this is what he would have wanted—
straightening up to light another Player's Navy Cut,
smoothing his mustache ends with the back of his hand.

A passage from the River Plate—I signed up
for Southampton, second mate on the tramp steamer Capella;
at the Cape Verde Islands where we put in for coal
Silva came aboard (we called him Long John), selling
perfumes, knickknacks, and was paid in Sunlight soap . . .

I tell myself that at last we were friends
as I reel back aboard after drinking in the Ship,
make the window latches fast, batten down the hatches
of my skylights, lie down in the reek
of the years that I want back as the wind tugs harder
and listen to the room creak and strain at its moorings.

THE LONDON DISSECTOR

ART LOVERS
She wants to see Hyde Park, Trafalgar Square, the Tower.
Instead, in the Tate you lecture her for an hour
on Bacon's rawness, his grasp of Renaissance Rome,
of *the things that happen with two people in a room* . . .
(Almost all, these days, best forgotten. To forget,
you walk the streets, or drink; but streets bring back
the rooms things happened in, or might have, you forget—
an attic in Holland Park, a basement in Hackney. Back
to square one, the room above a shrub-lined square
in Pimlico, or was it Primrose Hill? She lay in black
bra and slip, still, not sleeping.—It's quite a scare;
so you try drinking. On the way to the pub, willows
through sunlit drifts of smoke weep their reflections
into water.—She buried her face in the pillows.
And important suddenly, her foreign inflections,
her stillness, her weeping. Do you get the picture yet?)

RHYMERS
It's called the *Cheshire Cheese,* but it's a *chophouse,*
you repeat and explain between mouthfuls; not a cheese shop.
A chop bleeds on your plate, and blood, in little eddies, swirls
towards the middle. Your soul, which *low culture has
    nourished,*
feels at home here (though *you are too many,* though
it's Fleet Street—not the place *where Dr. Johnson flourished*
but where everything screams *Failure* at you . . .)
Was it in Borough you shared a mattress with two girls?
Lane after narrow lane, familiar—*Ma chère.*—
She's staying in one of the murky streets near Guy's.
You have a drink and start on *resurrection men*
and the *London Dissector;* read out the bit where he dies
coughing bright red, like your dear dead daddy; chain-

smoke, blub. You gape at a pair of red pants
draped—*a red rag to a bull, or danger*—on the chair
to dry, and this is the drooping soul of romance . . .

MARVELOUS BOYS
The packet boat is full of honeymooning couples
headed for your city of light; *how it gladdens us,*
you say, *to be traveling against the stream,*
makes us serious and strange to each other.
You chuff towards a cathedral filled with steam,
the current bears you on to a lodging house
in Camden Town (the landlady scares you more than Arthur),
French conversation lessons, fucking, quarrels, pubs.
You wake to the noise of all the churches in St. Pancras—
les voix d'enfants, chantant dans la coupole—
and would like to blow them sky-high. In a room full of
        mummies
at the heart of the tomb called the British Museum
you see a left foot that a rat has nibbled
and shiver: Africa. On the bus, punk rockers,
parodies of *him:* spike hair, a safety pin through a nipple,
a girl with shaved head and (she shows you) green pubes.

WHITECHAPEL
She tried on an old dress of her mother's; you wrote
(this was in your *First Love* phase), It's strange,
the way they dress each other for the sacrifice.
But now you name names, theories, candidates who range
from lunatics to royalty; Gull, your favourite . . .
You want to trace each doorway, entry and courtyard
where one of "five unfortunates" was drawn and quartered,
the final, blood-flecked, sweating room, the festoons
he hung around it, made of her intestines,
the banner of meat, bleeding; the ruined face
and always the stark white body spread on grey
mattress ticking, on a narrow bed of stains . . .

She is open, vulnerable; you drag up the soaked stones
of Smithfield, *meat-cathedral*, running full tilt into an aisle
of grinning heads (why do you dabble in this?); your sickly
    smile,
she's scared, she wants—better you went home, you agree.

NINETIES
Remember nights you breezed into the Café Royal
for gins and absinthes with the poetry crowd,
poured wine and *bons mots* down Lydias and Giselles?
Then tottered back, weeks later, muzzy, to your rooms
through a *Nocturne* by Whistler, turned up wicks on lamps
and penned a few impressions in tetrameter, with rhymes?
(You favoured ABBA.) The girls were all gazelles;
London was a gaslit heaven, a *flower that, at last*
like Dante's rose, opens to the moonlight, soft
as a yielding breast when whalebone is unlaced—
Good, that. Morning, and the pile of envelopes and stamps,
a hock-and-seltzer, then: *My dear Symons/Dowson/Gosse* . . .
(They're all dead, stupid: gone where everyone goes,
the scribblers and the muses, ash in a slow sift.
Who writes letters now? Get down the Cow & Crud
with Mick and Kevin, for a pint of something *real*.)

LATE SHOW
You go to Lauren's place—she makes Bucks Fizz,
you snort a line or two—and then it's out for eats,
your usual, the Romantica, where everyone *knows*.
But something's wrong. The single long-stemmed rose
you sent a week ago stares back from the primitive vase;
its long stem has become the shortest fuse.
When you were postgrads (Lauren's nineteenth-century lit.,
M.A. Harvard) you shared a kitchen, *just like Keats*
and Fanny (shy looks when you met in the hall);
she was always there to go to from the bluestocking drawl . . .
Now it's black sheets, a penthouse view of blazing blocks,

of masts and rigging in a hundred dry historic docks.
Does she think, *Will he ever learn where to find my clit*
or does she think (you do) you're boyish, witty, wise?
She's fuelled up for one of your more memorable rows.
Petal by petal, silently, you eat the rose.

POÉSIE DE DÉPARTS
Five minutes from your flat, alongside the canal,
a pub where you're not known. Trees are skeletons round
        here
but sunlight butters up the stucco, ignites houseboats, canal
(what was it you couldn't say?). You sip your beer
and think of her (she couldn't sleep); then you walk on—
the slant of rippling light on bricks, on moss and ferns
under bridges, is enough to bring you to your knees
(*O la rivière dans la rue*); another pub, another beer.
There was that freckled back and shoulder blade some-
        where—
Blackheath, Bloomsbury? And some nights were
        Camberwell's—
Camberwell was white skin, soft skin, pitch-black hair.
You sit awhile and drink, frown at the *canaille,*
drowned in dreams and burning to be gone—
watch them as they go, that one holds a furnace
in her walk—then come back to these four white walls
to look for lost connections on your hands and knees.

ALARM

For Alex

I was shaken at four
not by a footstep,
not by sirens in the street
and not by a scream
from the flat next door,
or a curt knock
at my own door,
but by my dream,
which drenched the sheet
and woke me to stare
at the glowing face
of a digital alarm clock
that was one more scare,
that would not stop
its silly, silent farce
of adding number to number,
patiently, mindlessly
totting up the score
in a sort of game
that I couldn't remember,
till the meaning was clear
of both the dream and this,
this new-smelling fear,
and nothing would be the same
as I'd hoped or wanted,
and I had to bring back,
name by lost name,
each word, caress or kiss
expended on me
since the whole thing began:
so many hours, lost hours,
lost on sofas, floors,

on piles of coats at parties,
on beds and lawns and beaches
under different stars,
struggling with panties,
skirts pulled up, on stairs,
on mattresses in cold rooms,
on the backseats of cars;
floozies, flowers,
salesgirls, Sloanes,
typists, teachers,
barristers, barmaids,
air hostesses, airheads,
princesses, PRs,
managers, mums—
they all came back
from wherever they'd gone,
and I couldn't pass the buck
and couldn't escape
into booze, or another
woman's body, a shape
I knew, woman smells,
eyes closing, moans;
they all had strange smiles,
and some were reproachful
and some apologetic,
but I couldn't tell who
had killed me, or whom
I had killed, or whether
I was hunter or hunted,
pimp or punter,
convicted man or screw;
or what I was to do
with each new coachful
of pain and anesthetic,
Kleenex, pills, address book,
too many vodkas, rums,
a torn dress, a broken shoe.

MOHICAN

Nothing, nowhere, he was tiny,
playing soldiers in the backyard,
when his salesman father sent him
picture postcards—London, England:
Big Ben, Hampton Court, the Hilton.
Later on, his father left them,
mother, son; she hit the bottle,
he dropped out and started drifting—
classic story. But the upshot?—
He had never learned discretion
is the better part of valor,
heard a war was there for winning,
and enlisted as a soldier . . .
Now he lives in London, England,
working as a barman, bouncer,
heavy, in a club in Soho;
works out daily, builds his body
to a hard and handsome weapon,
shaves his skull in a Mohican,
stripe of hair left down the middle—
frightens even his employers,
but they like that; he is a black belt,
martial arts, can kick like Bruce Lee,
kill a man with just two fingers.
Outwardly, though, he is gentle,
buys rice wine and veg for stir-fry
at the Chinese supermarket;
daytimes, in the park, does tai chi,
graceful, limpid; has read *Zen and*
(weird) *the Art of Motorcycle*
Maintenance, also *Despatches;*
watches in a daze those movies—
Taxi Driver, some new westerns—
where the white man is the loser.

Here he is in tracksuit, trainers,
riding on the London subway—
so why *is* he staring, wide-eyed,
trembling, sweating, at the Asian
student opposite, who fidgets,
full of unease, turns to whisper
to her friend—both young, both lovely,
T-shirts printed *Save the Forest*—
in a tongue he recognizes?

*

*"The first time the Americans came
they gave the children sweets to eat—
we didn't know their language, but they said* Okay,
and so we learnt that word, Okay.

*The second time, we gave them water to drink.
They didn't say anything, that time.*

The third time, they killed everybody."

GREENHEART

We came on them stretched out in a clearing,
feet and hands hacked off, privates in their mouths;
the gaudy shrieks beyond their blood-blocked hearing
with the echoes of their screams, the shots' aftermath—
I'd heard the loud black apparatus rise
and flap back, like the beating of giant moths
and bats that filled the ballroom with their cries
when Harry shouldered his way into a decade's
shuttered darkness at the Hotel de la Cruz—
the clapping hung, like flies on half-decayed
faces, in the still, hot blur of trees,
in thick green folds of forest . . . Then *OK, dickheads,*
keep your hands where I can see them. Freeze!
—the tone of the P.E. master's loutish sneer—
came from behind us, and in twos and threes
they loped from the bush, each a human snare
that bristled with knife, machete, automatic weapon;
jungle rig, stubble-shadowed face, a smear
of mud or blood on the cheekbones, sort of warpaint;
red-eyed, blank looks. I was sure we'd had it
there and then, but the tallish leader, wiping
sweat from his forehead, skull—he was shaven-headed
under the green kepi—studied us in turn
through narrowed eyes; grim-mouthed, grave, he nodded
to the others, made a new sound (stern
but less sadistic than resigned), and trekked
with the slackly slouching gait of a Soho slattern
towards the thicket, the overgrown green track
out of that killing ground. I was to follow,
I gathered from the goading of the gun at my back,
and so were Hugh and Harry; but Hugh, poor fellow,
whipped round with a reflex of anger—stupid, brave,
say what you like, both of them sound hollow—
and jabbed at his tormentor. Curses, brief

and terrible, rang out; a machete flashed, bright, cold;
Hugh's lean young body, come to grief,
fell forward, spurting blood; twitched and lolled;
and bouncing once, like a coconut at a fete,
mouth working soundlessly, his blond head rolled
in its own red carpet to my feet.

Permission to bury him was curtly refused.
After four days' hard going in the bush
we came to a stockade—not knowing what we faced:
gun emplacements, dogs; the plunge and thresh
of helicopters; acrid smoke from fires;
shouting men. *Looks like a frantic bish,*
said Harry, grinning, but I saw his worst fears
stand out like fever on his drawn white face.
We staggered on, past Indians building pyres
and heaping corpses on them—it seemed the place
had come under attack—then we were shoved
into a sort of shooting lodge-cum-palace,
a well-appointed bungalow. We shaved,
showered and shat, and were summoned to a room
in which a careful harmony had been achieved
between the hunting trophies and the views of Rome,
the birds in cages, flecks of glazed green fire,
and the rings on the fingers of the man on the sofa drinking
    rum.
One of his hands abstractedly kneaded the fur
at the neck of a chained leopard—though its chain
looked endless, it looped, in fact, as far
as a sticky mound of red meat (that had been Chan,
a Chinese associate, we were later told)
in the yard, and back to rest beneath the chin
of our host, to tangle with his chest hair. "Gold,
gentlemen" (he noticed that my eyes
had lit on it), "like much I own, solid gold.
I'm sure you're curious as to how—otherwise
you would not be here—how I came by . . . *all this.*"

(He gestured vaguely.) "I could tell how it was
in the beginning, the streets, the gangs, the genesis
of the killer in the college kid—but shit, man,
what would you make of it? A piece of piss
like you . . . Kicks and money're all of it, man,
I just loved the work. Once you've cut one throat
you can cut another, you're a hit man.
They saw me, they knew they were under threat.
Contract stuff. *Not murder, but a sacrifice*—
who said that? Some poet . . . I put them through it.
But the big deal was cocaine, the rich man's vice.
For a while, I smuggled emeralds as a front—
a front! White gold. Emeralds. Snow. Green ice.
Hollywood, New York, a million suckers on the hunt
for the big blow, happy trails—I've seen grown men
so high, they were packing some chick's cunt
with coke and eating it right out again.
She weren't complaining . . . Like business, I got big,
built some factories, airstrips, this place—then
I trained an army, bought a local bigwig
(I blew away the ones I couldn't buy)
and settled in. I mean to stay. And when some pig
from another setup, when the CIA, FBI
or DEA want to waste me, like
they tried at dawn today—well, they'll die
but not too quickly: out back there's a lake
full of alligators, and you've met Ramón,
my colonel with the Yul Brynner look
(he gets a kick from feeding pussy on
the bodies he can cut up still alive
and panting to be let go, until they're gone).
Sure, I've got some problems right now, I've
got the military sitting on my tail
and though I've spent enough to earn the people's love
some still prefer the Marxist's way of toil—
guerrillas (that's *gorillas*) in the hills—
would you believe some mercenary, some big tool

from London, England, thought he'd pay his bills
by picking up a contract on me? *Shit!*
Soon I'll have kids, out of their heads on crack or pills
I've sold them, coming here to make a hit . . ."

That evening, over dinner—some rich stew
of fish and fowl (for, though we had not seen
the grey-brown, sepia river, it was nearby, we knew)
and the fruits of that breeding fume of green,
the bush; and manioc; and beer and bitter coffee—
I agreed, though with an inward groan,
to tell how we had come out here, all three,
in search of something; how an item in the *Times*
had mentioned Harry's father, a missionary
who vanished without trace in troubled times
while trying to spread the gospel of the one true faith
at a trading post on the Xingu (teams
of anthropologists, explorers, men of pluck and pith
had failed to find him, failed to bring back word);
how Hugh, prizewinning author of *The Shining Path:*
Peru at the Crossroads, specialist reporter, heard
that crackdowns in Colombia, cartels at war
meant all the old distinctions were now blurred
and, commissioned by *Time-Life* (one-off, he swore)
and the *Telegraph,* hopped on the next plane;
how, listening one Christmas to my mother's endless store
of reminiscence, I had idly formed a plan
to make my way from Somerset to Guyana
and find my uncle's old greenheart plantation,
abandoned when the *British* went out of *Guiana;*
how, finally, before we had pulled back, as
each one would, the curtain of lianas,
creepers, wrecked vines, tendrils, leaves—our trackers,
bearers, guides looking fathomlessly on—
we had met up at the country club in Caracas
and dined with Reading, ex-consul, ex-con,
old colonial hand and classicist,

poet, small-hours philosopher who when far gone
in drink, as he most often was, would insist
on holding forth in loud hexameters;
how he told us in this way (though pissed)
that we might find (his utterance, always terse,
bordered on the cryptic here) *what all men seek*
somewhere up-country, a place, *though none of it matters*
except at a purely personal level, that men forsake,
where birds cry out in pain, and nature suffers a curse.
"So we joined forces, bade farewell to that old soak
and came, weeks later, to the Hotel de la Cruz."

At this our host's eyes widened. "And you found . . . ?"
"Nothing," I went on, "but an empty shell,
a building sinking back into the ground,
reclaimed by jungle, the husk of a hotel."
"That's all?" "Except that, in an upstairs room,
when Hugh broke down the door, a voice croaked *Well.*
You're here at last. We peered into the gloom
and saw a man cross-legged on a bed,
caked in bat shit; then he seemed to loom
up, a skeleton with dark enormous head
and yards-long, thick white beard. *I knew you'd come.*
O'Hanlon's the name, this apparition said,
but call me Redsie. Have some peanuts. Rum?
He reached behind him, and—I promise you—
unplugged a bottle from his bony bum.
I gasped and turned and ran and, shouting, Hugh
and Harry followed, half-falling over themselves.
And that was all we found there, but for bats, and two
huge wooden boxes, stacked on shelves
in the foul-smelling kitchen; and in these,
plump white plastic packets, pillows for elves.
All three of us round the boxes on our knees—
Hugh split one packet, sniffed and tasted. Sort of snuff,
I thought, and like snuff it made me sneeze.
Hugh, I noticed, put a packet of the stuff

in his rucksack when we left, alarmed by each
(*Off the tee,* said Harry, *and into the rough*)
shrill shriek and squawk and sudden screech,
the noise of treetop colonies, the mechanical shout
of birds and insects in their meshed arcades, the creatures
of loud hot light and silent, cool damp shade;
we saw only trees and scrub, heard dense flocks fly up
whenever one of us stopped to take a shot:
unbroken walls of green, green waterfalls that flow up—"

"You had already entered my . . . kingdom," our host put in,
and I was silent. Helpless fury welled up, sank.
I looked at him, a great distorted grin.
"Most entertaining. Thank you. But who is it I thank?
My name is Silvano, alias Silva. You are . . . ?"
He extended his jewel-encrusted hand. "Bowerbank,
Gavin Bowerbank. This is Harry Ormerod-Carr,
and our young friend, my cousin, so ruthlessly cut down,
was the Honorable Hugh Greenwood. I might go so far
as to challenge you to give me some redress at dawn
for his life, with weapons of your choice—" *"My choice?!"*
—"if I did not know you for a bully and—since what's done
isn't even by your hand—a coward." I'd raised my voice;
now I quietened once again. In a flash, Silvano,
who was sallow olive, turned a livid green; high voice
the more menacing for sounding *molto piano,*
he said, "On the contrary, my friend, I'll meet you
to settle this in six hours' time. I'll . . ." (almost soprano)
"fight you with machetes, and I'll beat you.
I'm not some Indian or Ladino scum,
some piece of shit—I'll have Raoul cook and eat you
for what you've said; and, since it's clear we've come
to the end of talking, I'd like to let you know
just how deep you're mixed up in this jungle scam,
Mr. Fuckin' Nose-in-Air, Mr. Do-No-
Evil, Speak-No-Evil, Ass-in-Fuckin'-Hell."
I reeled back, flabbergasted. *"Numero uno,*

you think it was so great for the guys your uncle
bought and sold? You think they loved him for the way
he took their land, their women and their lives? He'd sunk all
he had in greenheart, so he had to make it pay;
then inside two years he'd sunk all that in booze
and crazy expeditions, looking for *le pays
d'or,* Eldorado; found the Hotel de la Cruz
instead, shipped down the widows and the daughters of
the men he'd killed (the ones he couldn't use)
and started cashing in. The place was like a sieve:
full of holes, through which dirt and riches poured—
enough spunk was spilled in it to save
the human species from extinction (some were spared
and brought up to their mothers' trade; some not).
He'd taken everything, and now he took their spirit
from the trees, the greenheart he left to rot."

(Through all this Harry and I sat, stunned,
astonished, almost stupefied.) With that he stood:
"Since you're my guests, I now invite you to get stoned,
just like the Preacher. You're surprised? That stud,
your uncle, did all he could to populate the place
but he had help—every little half-caste bastard
belonged to Unc, or else to his accomplice,
your daddy, Carr; well, you've all met him . . ."
This latest information seemed to nonplus
Harry, seemed, in fact, to find him not at home.
"The old man turned up there one day, the hotel,
looking pretty bad, raving, *the Indians would get him*
if the flies and fever didn't, some half-assed tale
of how, at his one-horse mission not far from the coast,
the people had begun to die—*A quiet hell,
influenza, smallpox, these things are the cost
for them*—those were his words — and when his crucifix
and prayers and Bible failed to save them, they had cursed
their new god and prepared to offer up a sacrifice—
him—to the old . . . But he escaped when Muldoon,

a defrocked priest who used to trade in sassafras,
heard of his trouble and strapped him to a mule . . .
At the hotel he got his mind back—half of it, at least;
took three wives: *Left Leg, Right Leg, Middle One,*
and may the Spirit of the Rum be blest,
Cassiri and the Coca leaf be blest— that was his creed—
O mulier multitudinis: man, he was a blast.
Life in that hotel was . . . a little *crude,*
if you take my meaning; in time they all checked out,
your uncle Greenheart (he was called that by his crowd
of sex slaves—he was hard and, when he was chicked out,
crazy, but he could bend) along with the rest;
the Preacher hung on in there like a chigoe
when it gets under your skin. He rides the crest
of a cocaine wave—the place is useful to me now—
and takes himself for some fool Jesus Christ
or some explorer my men killed. So what's new?"

He turned and left us. Neither of us spoke
as we were escorted to our sleeping quarters
(we declined saltcellars of white snuff). A spark
from a match, some curt, unpleasant-sounding orders
and I was alone in darkness. I can't believe I slept
(imagine for yourself my state of mind), but from the borders
of sleep I started up as a shadowy figure slipped
inside the wire-meshed door (mosquitoes in a whining cloud,
the whirring fan); bare feet distinctly slapped
on concrete; I lay as if manacled,
cat's-eyes, an unfamiliar smell came through the air
and a woman loomed above me, scantily clad.
Her face curved down to mine, I felt her hair
fall around me like a curtain—and she whispered low:
"This may be your last chance. We'll be OK here,
they won't disturb us. What you don't already know
I'll teach you; and I'll do anything you want."
She touched my cheek; took my hand, placed it below
the brown-blue blotch of a nipple. "I'd r-rather you w-went,"

I stammered as she moved it slowly down her stomach
until it touched—"And what if I won't?"—
a firm, round, glistening, smooth hummock,
damp fuzz beneath that. I wiped my sweat-drenched eyes
with my other hand, tried to sit up in the hammock
(a mistake); she smiled, defiant, mischievous but wise
beyond her years, her taunting stare. "I'll call the guard."
"You idiot. First he'd fuck me, two, three ways,
then force you to fuck me too. You're getting hard"—
she put her hand on me—"See? Call him, and watch
what happens, or better still, enjoy my gourd."
She took her fingers off me—I could feel myself twitch—
and thrust them into her black tuft; rocked to and fro.
My eyes fixed on that jungle, "Are you a witch?"
I asked. She laughed, a long laugh, deep and free.
"A witch? No, but I'm here to cast a spell."
Her head dipped, warm wet engulfed me, I read *Ro-
sa-de-Fon-se-ca* on her back . . . I was about to spill
but pulled away. "I can't make you want this,"
she said; "you're pretty weird. Silvano'll spoil
that face of yours, like he does" (now more a hiss
than human speech) "with everything." This was the voice
of experience, no doubt. "But, for one kiss—
I'll help you get away from here." Spawned in vice
and raised in it, schooled in Miami, Bogotá—
the fleshpots and perspiring tropic dives—
she was offering to save my life. I looked at her
and saw two doves fly up from their armpit-roosts;
her hidden folds and clefts now seemed to utter
not a musky otto, but attar. "My future rests,
madam, not in your hands but in my own;
not on your favors, between your legs or breasts,
but in the strength and courage I have always shown
a world too heedless of itself to keep from harm."
She bent close again, and I saw both eyes shine
like a tiger's, but with a kindly light; she raised her arm
and crossed the air above me; then she stooped

for a third and final time, and placed on my wrist a charm,
a bracelet she slid from the slim wrist it *had* looped.
"This will protect you when you face your enemies"
(a dreadful cry pierced the thin partition); tight-lipped,
I took it (a drawn-out sob). "First, the enemas.
Then they'll have their fun with him—your friend Harry—
and then they'll have more fun, with him *and* me.
It all gets filmed. Please don't be in a hurry
to help him—you can't, no one can." She was gone.
I staggered, reeling, blinded, to a chink—the horror!—
Harry, two guards and the girl, one flesh; a gun
in Harry's mouth, Harry in hers . . . My pounding blood
kept time with the blows the guards began
to rain; a buzzing screech, a blade; everything was blood.

I must have fainted—when I next saw day
a huge paw was shaking me. One thought—
"This is the day on which I am to die"—
went through my mind, and shortly after that
I faced Silvano, spruce in his green fatigues,
both of us armed to the teeth, at
the appointed place and time. My own togs
were pretty well in tatters—I must have made
a sorry sight; I noticed he wore dog tags
(though gold ones) in paramilitary mode,
and recalled the bracelet. Fired by that memory
I advanced on him and died there in the mud—
though what transpired was this: stock-still, marmoreal,
he offered his thick neck, his swart head;
I offed it in three swipes; his next bit of mummery
froze my blood and stopped my heart. For instead
of toppling, calmly he bent and picked up by the hair
his own head; holding it at arm's length, stood
upright; turned it on me—did I truly see and hear
these things?—and, as if it had been
a pumpkin lantern (though it glowed with an eerie
greenish light and dripped stuff that was *green*)

he was clutching, and the whole episode
no more than a foolish prank at Halloween,
he held his ground as the lips creaked open, said:

"What can you still stand to know? How fast the forest
is burning up, what cattle on the cattle farms are forced
to eat—which you then eat, hamburger-head? First

the white men fucked the Indians, and we're still fucking them.
Oh yes, they'll learn our principles of trade, in time.
It's not as if we've ever worked together as a team.

But one law behind all this, one lord of misrule;
one lord of the flies, of the virus (this is real),
of the flying fish and of us—instinctive, visceral;

you learnt it once, forgot it. Now learn that my name
will start you on the right track to the truth that I am—
more than rum or yoppo, that truth will make you numb.

Greenheart, Greenmantle, Greenaway, Harry, Hugh:
I'm all these, and Silvano; and Beelzebub too;
and Bertie Lake, bullion-robber on the run. And you.

You look amazed, and rightly. I'm not peddling tapas.
This trickster's games have tripped up jaguars and tapirs
and I traffic with the lives of tribes, of rubber tappers.

Follow the trail back through the undergrowth, the trees,
through the prizes, record times and dazzling tries,
the rowing fours, the summer-evening centuries—

into something blacker than a black fruit's rind,
than a negro's skin, into the ramifying, overgrown
forest of yourself, into the rambling, ruined

hotel rooms you call your mind, looped brilliance
and glooms, where you are constantly arraigned
for your desire to dominate, to keep your head, to hold your
   own.

Aged ten: *tingling with pride, hot with luck, you laid*
out, on a bed of cotton wool, under a perspex lid,
a thrush you found flopped in a dusty corner
of the playground. It would be the star turn
on Parents' Night—Nature Club had the whole back wall!
Next day, you were smug, smiling all the way to school,
but as you bounded into the classroom you felt small,
frightened; something had gone wrong. A nasty smell
thickened as you went nearer, made you retch—
and there, instead of the soft, plump, speckled swell
of its breast, maggots tumbled over themselves,
a grey mush. You whirled round, knocking jars off shelves;
pondweed, larvae and spawn spilled in a viscid pool
with tadpoles, water boatmen, a terrapin at full stretch . . .
Eight: *heraldic, the stag beetle never stood a chance*
in your kangaroo court, nor the humble worm.
You yanked one's antlers out; chopped the other into bits
which you then pinned to the earth with nails
the better to watch them wriggle and squirm.
Their sufferings magnified you, little, afraid
of everything. You pulled apart two copulating snails,
intrigued by the white, capped member like a length of string,
then crunched them underfoot. You felt strong
as you broke off daddy longlegs' long legs one by one,
tied a firework to a dog's tail and took bets
on how much it would leave, or trapped a spider you'd named
   Fred
under a magnifying glass and left them in the sun.

Make for Paradise Island, tell your tale and then keep silent."

FROM
HARM

NOCTURNE

When young couples loving
beneath the unleaving
chestnut trees in Holland Park
fill me with loathing
of those who unclothing
lie wetly together in the dark,

when every good intended
like the harm unmended
is stripped and flayed by sodium light,
all that I've kept hidden
comes back unbidden,
and nothing, now, will be all right.

VISITING

He visited, the man who takes your life
and turns it upside down, from floor
to ceiling; and he saw I had no wife,
and saw the things that I had worked hard for
and smiled, as if he knew what went on *here*.

He visited the corner of my flat
where daily I had spooned out food
for my dainty-footed, air-sniffing cat
and through the summer, chunks left half-chewed
had poured rich smells into the atmosphere.

Flies visited the smells. They hung in heat
like helicopters seen from a distance,
they drooled and fed on rotting processed meat,
they laid their eggs. The buzzing small insistence
should have warned me, the cat not going near.

Friends visited, but no one noticed anything.
And when he tore my carpet up, the man—
No lie, I nearly puked my ring.
I saw yellow-white seethe in a silver can
full of dank sawdust, a towpath by a weir—

I visited my father on the bank
where he and I went fishing each weekend;
the shrubs, the weir, the lock and river shrank,
our bicycles had vanished round a bend
and a high tide taken all our gear.

I visited my father in the pubs
where I had watched him drink away the hours
of talk or silence, piling up the stubs
in ashtrays, but the cigarettes were sour
and the bitter had an aftertaste of fear.

I visited my father by the sea
where he had scrubbed me with a gritty towel
and held me till I squirmed and struggled free;
I heard the gulls scream and the sea wind howl,
the freezing water writhed and flung me clear.

I visited my father in his grave
and grubbed until I found all that was left—
a matchbook of maggots. *Grieve, grieve*
they whispered when I held it aloft,
Grieve, grieve when I put it to my ear.

THIRTY-FIVE

WINDOW BOX
You've come to this, your square of dark at rooftop level,
a square of light, a window box—hers;
she busies herself in the kitchen while your grinning devil
slowly mists over. Everything blurs.

Hurrumph. You swipe a porthole clear.
Not funny anymore: the patience of a saint
and her pottering have taken on
new purpose. Beddy-byes. You watch her disappear

through a wall, but you caught the scent
that time she loomed at the top of her bathroom stair,
a startle of white, a fuzz of hair . . .
Tonight, though, it's been hours and all she's done

is pour glass after glass of wine, hide her face
in her upturned hands as if resting her case
and sob. Anyway, her shoulders shake.
Earlier, you had a nasty shock—

she stood at the sink abstractedly washing a cup
and seemed to see you when she looked up:
peered as if the glowing point of your cigarette
was your eye, so fiercely

you'd been staring, and so long. The farce
that goes on night after night in secret—
your shyly peeping round the edge
of the window frame, clutching the window ledge.

TEA

A stranger thumbing through the obvious books,
the often-noticed tilt of her head
as she dangles a tea bag in the vortex,
a phantom imprint on the bed,
a perfume trace, the ghost of one blond hair;
between her tooth and lip, a thin saliva thread,
her bra and slip, almost, slung on your chair . . .

The spoor of watch and earrings in the inch-thick dust.
The cream-or-lemon stain on the duvet. (You must
clean up this place, you must clean up your act.)

You've come to this, accessory after the fact.

MOTHS

That night I came home late and found
a moth flickering helplessly round and round
inside the lampshade. I went to help it.

The sixty-watt bulb had not shriveled it
but its wings were scorched,
it was beyond help, almost beyond harm.

As it unwound slowly on my outstretched palm
it left a powdering of gold dust
as fine as the blusher that streaked my T-shirt

where her cheekbone had brushed it,
its wing beat was as powerful and as fragile
as the blink of an eyelash in the half-inch

of smoky air between us.
We'd sat as strangers lately introduced,
we'd chewed the fat and made a date for lunch

and my heart was fluttering when I asked her
to dance to an old one by Elvis.
It was tricky but she was lithe and agile

and had just fitted her pelvis
to mine when suddenly—someone had seen us,
she had to, she was sorry but, she was leaving.

Where's the harm? I wondered as, stood stewing
in my own body heat in a crowd of couples
melted together, I watched her bobbing and weaving

towards the powder room. I left soon after.
In the taxi I thought, nothing doing,
this one's too hot to handle,

don't make that lunch, it's not worth the candle . . .
Next day I read, among other troubles,
that the place had been torched—

it seemed someone paid through the nose
for a deal that wasn't up to snuff, the upshot:
three women trapped in the Ladies' choked to death

and were done to a turn. I caught my breath.
The moth had taken so long to die, God knows,
that in the end I crushed it.

COBH

At East Ferry a boat's ribs curve out of blackened mud
like the blackened skeleton of a whale;
farther down the coast road the docks are derelict,
the windows of sheds are smashed and on a weed-sprouting
    wall
someone has sprayed INTERNMENT KILLS; the broken derrick
and the rusting gantry loom prehistoric and mad
in the evening sky. You stand on one of the wharves
and look into the oily grey-brown waters of Cobh
and see a crab groping through a porthole like a cave
where brass is barnacle-encrusted and the sea grass waves
to itself in the mirror that is turning back to sand
and a chandelier still gleams through the murk
when the camera catches it and shoals of fish shoot away
    from the sound
of the bathyscope as it bumps and scrapes along the Plimsoll
    mark.

SHIP OF FOOLS

How were they led to water, to chartering the leaky boat—
Old twin berth, twelve knots, no mast or sail, no swivel chair:
Less than what you'd want, say, for a weekend's pottering
    around
In a tributary of the Teme, where you *could* run aground,
Drop anchor in a kiddies' paddling pool, or scare
A shoal of minnows, or capsize a boy's bobbing float—
Young men who in their daily lives oozed savoir faire,

Even under pressure, always knowing what was what?
Rescue them, can't we, from whatever brought them here,
South of everything they knew, to chance a fishing trip, a
Brothel and a salty bar, a boat without a skipper;
Opened them to influences of the tropics; showed them fear;
Amazed two stomachs shriveled tightly to a single knot,
Then burst their lungs with blackness? No, it's written in the
    plot,

In the stars they could not read, in the pride their natures felt
Shrugging off the obstacles to things they chose to do,
Forcing all the world to grant their every slightest wish,
On the cutting edge of options, in the blind pursuit of fish;
United on this, that whatsoever they projected, few—
None, that's to say—objected to. No deal undealt,
Dirty trick untried, no shit unheaped on someone's dish . . .

*

They had drifted half a world from Cape Halfalump
While one of them tried to coax the fuel pump
Or untangle the screw, the rudder-thing, and the other sot
Made a meal of fish heads and blood smells and sat
Entranced by the click-click of his ratchet and his line
Nonchalantly winking in the sun. Then they were alone,
Massively, with the fish for company and something brewing

In the sky like a wet bruise, the slap of waves, the boat
      slewing
Sideways onto them, tiny, slung between two green-mauve
Spires of a sea cathedral that was on the move.
Imagining the worst (and some imaginings are true),
Not knowing yet what it would be, they went below to try
Getting through with *Mayday* or an SOS—the radio-ham
      thing—
But neither of them knew how to work the damn thing.

Every hour that went by took them farther from help;
Lower and lower came the sky, the sea rose like an Alp;
In no time, their few supplies were washed, yo-ho-ho,
Easily overboard, merrily bobbing as water sloshed, yo-ho, o-
Ver the gunwale, round the deck and back to its, yo-ho, h-
Eaving, sliding lair. At last it was still, but no one cried *Ahoy!*;
Dead calm, empty, flat horizon. Days. *Swim for it.*

Did they know, now, what was coming, and did they fear it?
Rudderless; the paintwork blistered, cracked;
Outboard flooded: thus they found the boat, with seven
      crooked
Weals scratched in the fiberglass, no fishing gear,
No clothes, nothing, not a trace of Garth or Greer
Except for hanks of their hair—they had tied hooks to these,
Dangled them, watched fish take them and break them with
      ease.

ART HISTORY

FISH MARKET, VENICE,
BY SOPHIE MACPHERSON
You remember your first great arrival in Venice—
at the fish market, gold and silver scales
fell from your eyes

and into your pockets. A doubloon hoard.
You remember your first shared, shuttered bed-and-board,
the dresser crisscrossed by a thousand little snails.

You remember the black curls
on her mound of Venus,
the tracks of two snails strung like pearls.

VELVET
A room in Venice where our differences could be aired:
William Morris hangings, pearl-rich brocades,
a Fortuny dress brought out from under wraps
(she was Sybil Sassoon—in Orpen's portrait—to the life . . .)

So, our luck was in. Her small cry of relief
when I met her in rainy darkness at the station—
unmolested, she had crossed the barricades
carrying her huge valise, her superstition.

Years before, two soldier boys had marched her
from a train to a hut in a railway siding.
Between us lay the bayonet that had marked her.
"There's so much hate. I can't live in hiding . . ."

She shuddered at the Massacre of the Innocents.
We scared each other recalling *Don't Look Now*
and saw blood seeping out of every wall. "No,
I can't go back . . . I have to . . . It's *insane*."

When, a year later, she was "running from all that"
on a tourist visa and her nerves, I met her at the airport—
she was an undesirable . . . And when she found Sophie's
Fish Market, Venice hanging in my poky flat,

with red flags—those great red drapes—
billowing on the colonnade, she stared, and stared . . .
Moving on, to Paris, Fontainebleau, "somewhere . . . *apart*"
she left a crushed-velvet one-piece among my trophies.

MISSING

Messages. The dumb machine's small bright red eye
is blinking on and off, and I'm home and dry—
the cat uncurls and looks up, stretching, yawning
in a wedge of light between the windowsill and broken blind,
the grey-blue light of five-thirty in the morning . . .
The blue light was my blues, the red light was my mind . . .
Another half an hour and the adult video begins
once more behind my bloodshot, sleepless eyes:
is it lifesaving, wrestling? Everybody wins, she pushes him
        away
but only to clutch him closer, surprise, surprise,
no dream-stewardess is offering me coffee, though it's day
coming red-eyed over the roofs, over the rim
of the world, bringing for me cat's breath, for her: him.
                          *
Underachieving, Underground-haunting, I descended to
a twilit flickering world, as I'd been led to expect;
I followed with my eyes the lighted windows rattling past
and found you out in one of them, moving too fast
for a sound to leave my open mouth. Could I detect
some sadness on your face, beautiful, downcast?
What assignation drew you on? There came a blast
of noise, a rush of foul air, a red light changed to green
somewhere far down the line, you did not look back,
and in your hurry to be moving, you had not seen
how in another second you'd be changing track . . .
If you are Eurydice, could I be Orpheus, I mean
could anything I might still say or sing reclaim you?
                          *
Return, rerun, a dream of moon-reflecting sea,
a neon beach bar, teenage crowd and glowing jukebox,
the screen alive with ghosts, the comical dubbed voices
and the couples sitting, knees drawn up on the sand;
we are drifting away from them, close and slow,

not talking, arms around each other's shoulders lightly—
the whole day's heat has soaked into our itching backs ...
We kiss, your tongue is warm and quick, but something stops
    you,
you break away and run towards the sea, you turn and
suddenly, remembering *It's not like years ago*
the fear of getting caught   the recklessness in water
a flash of white your little gasp and you are swimming
    brightly
away from me   the undertow *What if there were two*

                    *

Paris, and the boulevard I walked down with you
towards your mother's charming attic, your mother who
so charmingly stayed with friends while we played house
and fooled around; and here is the café where you sat
for me to take your picture, pouting *à la parisienne;*
here is the little bridge that crosses to the Ile St. Louis
where you clutched me—though we were already late
for our rendezvous, for the movie, everything—
and opened your lips and said, "Kiss me! On ze mouse!";
here are the old men by their bookstalls, regarding me
    strangely
for here I am weeping, remembering *St. Louis. Louis,* the Seine
cold-grey below, staring until one of them takes my arm
gently, and leads me nowhere, away from here, from harm.

                    *

Heroine of your teen romance, and so much a child
that when I called and found you swaddled on a sofa
in a kind of nappy (the "thing" had split, you'd been emptied
    out
and the blood and afterpain were all you had to suffer)
you could smile at me, a dazed and happy smile
as I fed you cakes and poured champagne—sweet things ...
We were celebrating, I was yours—why should you doubt?—
and had been since the night you shyly asked to stay,
unpeeled, unhooked, turned unhesitatingly

towards me, "trembling with excitement," as you later said;
no thought for the thing flushed down, away,
no thought for the world that wasn't you and me,
no thought, now, for me (sweet things he told you "turned
      your head").

                              *

You were quiet, in your bath, and you were going to sleep
      with him.
I knew it, the cat knew it. The bathwater felt it,
and the sliver of soap with which you soaped your quim,
the sponge with which you soaked your breasts, both smelt
      it—
when you clasped your nose and swiftly ducked
(sink or swim, you witch!), your hair waved like sea grass,
your thatch, laid flat like tangled seaweed, foam-flecked,
lifted on the swell, and a slither of eel-slick skin
showed like the pearl-pink inside of a shell . . .
You surfaced, shifted slightly, settled your arse.
I saw it clenching tightly as his fingers gripped,
I saw your sea anemone open, close as he plunged in.
Looking up, you smiled. I would say you slipped.

                              *

She moves on. She moves on,
taking with her when she's gone
your jacket, jeans and shirts,
your better self. It hurts and hurts.

She moves on. "What this place needs,"
she said when she first stayed the night,
"is a woman's touch."
And she gave it that all right—
books trashed, clogged hairs in the sink;
she scarred your back, kneed you in the crotch,
told you that you stank of drink,
stabbed you in the heart. It bleeds and bleeds.

She moves on. Into another world,
one in which you don't belong
and in which she never furled
her legs round yours, and the song
has changed, forever, and is wrong:
not "Marry me" or "Let's do it"
but "I want us to be friends."
And you can see right through it,
and it claws and claws, and never ends.

She moves on. Now what she thinks
is that you didn't love her, not enough,
and that he's "easygoing." And it's tough,
your wanting her. It stinks.

She moves on. She doesn't call,
she won't come back, she's too far in,
her love was as fake as her leopardskin,
as quickly shed. You fall and fall.

She moves on. Like a single cell,
like a virus, with as much in mind,
as much concern for what it leaves behind,
as much speed. And it's hell, it's hell.

*

Missing, believed lost, five-feet-four-and-a-half
of warm girl, of freckled skin and sulky laugh
and blood on the sheets and ash on the pillow
with the smell of bacon, eggs and lubricant—how that
    lingers—
for breakfast; crumpled things to scoop up from the floor
and press against my face, and cunt-smell on my fingers;
I'll skip the part about love it seems so silly and low
—the aftertaste of afternoons in a strange bed in a stranger's
flat, "I love the way you go down on me," breathless, "more.
Harder," and a red dress from the wardrobe, and the
    dangers:

at 3 a.m. your boot like a bad dream pounding on the door
and the way that anything you wanted could be true,
if you said it was. But not this. Missing. You.

                                    *

Over. It's over. Three words uttered matter-of-factly
that I hear over and over in the sound of the wheels
hissing through rain, pointed north, as I drift in and out of
        sleep
on the backseat, remembering our scenes, line by line, exactly
remembering line by line the words that tell you how it feels
to have brought this sadness with you from the womb
remembering *I could turn you inside out* on the car stereo
you swung like a handbag to our hotel room
and your body kneeling, bent double, face buried in the duvet,
remembering how I stayed awake all night to watch you sleep,
lips parted, eyelids flickering *She is so beautiful she is so
        young and Oh*
our drive next day through driving rain, our bickering
I can't stand this, give me "Les douleurs," give me Dufay

                                    *

Viera Lodge: a drystone wall and one bent tree
and nothing else between us and the boiling sea,
the slate-grey, roiling sea. The wind wails
and we are safe inside, drinking, hearing how
a boy from the island, nineteen, hanged himself for love
of a girl up for the holidays from Glasgow.
And suddenly, for no reason, or for love,
I see myself walking down the slight slope of lawn
in the awful slate-grey light of dawn,
the cat prowling round an empty flat, listening for the key
in the lock, racing after shadows; red sails
in the sunset, a profile in the prow—it's you—
a world away from where I lie, bloated, blue.

                                    *

Every move you make, every step you take—the "disco deck"
throbs, a blaze of glory as the evening flashes, fades;
waterlight flushes us, glass after glass brings back the blood

to day-defeated faces, each one doing its best
to hide a grey fatigue. You are not here, we flash and fade
as the loud, lit boat glides through London, I am obsessed—
in a small saloon, a scattering of couples watch the end
of *L'Atalante,* then *Ai No Corrida,* cries and whispers
      drowned
by the throbbing engine. You saw it with a girlfriend
and called to say, "I need you, now. Can I come round?"—
I turned you away. My stomach churns, I turn and wade
      through dreck
of bodies—every vow you break, every smile you fake—
that twist and writhe in water, clutch and clasp in mud.

         *

She came racing towards me, across a dance floor
littered with tables, bottles, petals; she wore a flower
behind her ear, her hair piled high on her head,
wisps falling carelessly; my child bride, my sweet
stamped her foot, one side then the other, flamenco-style,
gathered her skirt in both hands, by the hem,
and tugged it left, right, in time with her stamping feet;
raced towards me, zigzagged, in front of me, behind,
a challenge in her eyes and in her wide white smile . . .
It's crazy what you could have had, it's crazy what you could
      have had,
it seems a shame to waste your time to me—REM
remind me, I rewind, replay, I know by heart
that was just a dream Pause Stop *I need this* Start
         *

Now that I no longer sleep,
now I could no more count sheep
than the nights they spend together, or apart,
now I pray she'll have a heart
and come back, and come back,
now I stare into a black
and featureless night that goes on
and on, a grey and featureless dawn,
now that the telephone is quiet

and the memory runs riot,
now that I mix up the days
and am fuck-all use in several ways,
now that she's safely in the sack
with someone else, and won't come back,
now that I'm rotted through and stink
of loneliness, self-pity, drink,
now that she's finally taken off
and I'm left here to shake and cough
and wait for my first heart attack
or for her to wake up and come back,
now that no one wants to know
who I see, what I do or where I go,
now that more flee from me each week,
the women who sometime did me seek,
than I've had dinners on my plate,
now that her love has turned to hate
I think of this: the openhanded way I had
of slapping her, her lovely face, her head,
and making her see stars,
or pushing her downstairs
and out of the door. There's more—

*

Open me, the book says—*Cherokee,* by Jean Echenoz—
when I brush it, hunting for something else, and so I do,
and on the title page, an entry wound, black and yellow-
    brown,
the words "Hole by Murphy, summer 1991"—
the ash dropped from your cigarette, your head dropped in a
    doze
to your chest, and the paper burned right through
to page thirteen; the sun in Brittany burned down,
your head jerked upright from its dream, your face was
    flushed
and freckled, your plump pale arms and shoulders turning
    red—

had your mother seen, your aunt seen? They went on sipping
    tea
and talking. Was it that day you wrote *"Nom d'une pipe,*
tu me manques" and sent the postcard that flutters now from
    the book
you gave back sheepishly, unread? (Tearstains by Alan,
    1993.)

                            *

Night, the roof is leaking, and I perform my dance
with saucepan and bucket, and the steady drip, drip
of dirty water tells how love leaked out of my life;
for two years, I tried to stop the holes and fill the cracks
but there were always more, and the slow drip of slights,
insults, screaming on the telephone, hanks of hair
yanked out, left a stain that spread everywhere.
So now that the roof leaks, and the cat looks askance
at my attempts to catch as I would a second chance
these drops like huge tears falling from black heights,
I drink up regret, to the last drop,
and stop and let it all come down in cataracts
to drown me: night and rain and the thought of my not-wife.

PERSONAL

Tonight we have a game called "Bits and Pieces,"
in which she hands me some of his old loves
saying she wants me to have them. Silk scarves,
handkerchiefs. A silver hip flask. Halves
of plump fob watches, stopped in 1910.
The slender cigarette case, too slender for
my flavorless, filtered smokes. I smooth the creases
in a pair of dainty chamois leather gloves.

Some of them *his* mother handed on.
The rest are Shepherd's Bush and Chelsea Arts, prewar
Bohemian and dandyish. Except his dog tag,
indestructible, 1119681;
and this ring I always thought his wedding ring
but which he wore, she says, "for luck. A personal thing."

BAUDELAIRE

Two lovers, and that word, *infected.*
The red and black, black and red
of Hubert's boxes, a hundred pills in each.
The bravery in every word that's said,

in the small talk and the tall tales of Sylvia Beach
and the offhand epitaph for Christopher Cox,
"He's dead, of course, like everybody else."
The lucky life I've led.

The lucky life I've led
here, for three whole days,
not having thought once in all that time
of my rivals, of my wasted prime,

of her penchant for surprising herself,
her reaching for the bookshelf
above the bed
in the poky little box

above the rue de Rivoli—the smells
of smoke and sweat and semen, trapped air,
trapped lives—and reciting Baudelaire,
of his black and red

striped wallpaper and his darkened windows,
the black and red that filled his eyes
when it came to him that everybody dies
and that he would soon be dead,

her freckled shoulders shouting *Health,*
the toxic tears I shed,
my taking her by force and by stealth,
the venom I injected.

WEST 11TH STREET

for Bruno Fonseca

Night after starry New York night, I swung away from
    laughter
outside the White Horse, steered an uncertain course
to West 11th Street, dropped on all fours
and crawled up the creaking stairs to the great height
of the attic playpen, where I scribbled till first light.

I was missing Anna then, and night after
starry night, I conjured her from E. J. Bellocq's
Storyville Portraits, palming myself off
with one particular photograph.
And once, sweating bourbon, I emptied my bollocks

on the blanket, tonguing Sally S———'s cleft—
she'd rescued me from outside an East Village bar
where, lifted off my feet and just as suddenly unhanded,
I'd flown a little way, and landed
facedown on the rain-soaked sidewalk, cheek pressed to a
    star.

The attic's a nursery now, and not a trace is left
of all that carry-on and lah-di-dah, not a whiff
of beer breath, Camel-stench, not a snort or sniff
of bad cocaine, not a glimpse of a single starry night
anywhere in its innocent blue and white . . .

Back after six years, I sat round the kitchen table
with Richard and Elizabeth, and the talk avoided death
but I recalled how, the night before, you'd come in,
how the coat hung off your bones, how shockingly thin
your hair and beard were, and how each breath

rattled in your chest—you were "stable"
but everyone, yourself included, knew that soon, soon,
your beautiful El Greco face would be gone, your mother
mourning her son, and Isabel, Caio, Quina their brother;
the light in your eyes already looked as pale as the moon

in your lovely *"Casa i lluna,"*
your speech was slurred by drugs, and too slow
for us to take up our ten-year conversation about Caravaggio;
and sometimes, though trying to be there, you were elsewhere,
on your daily pilgrimage to the Met, in the blinding air

of the Zattere, painting through the starry nights of Barcelona
or thinner and thinner on your final bed . . .
And none of this, not Dick's best friend being dead,
not the thought that you would soon be dead,
not the paintings that would stay forever in your head,

made any sense; no more did it make sense
that my last words to you should be a lame "Take care,"
that I should see, as I said them to the telephone, your
        thinning beard and hair,
that I should climb through the starry night above Newark
towards a loved face, and all that uphill work,

that I should wake from a dream of innocence
to sunrise in the window and sun-dazzle on the wing
of the 747, a white floor below, and empty heaven the exact
        same blue
as the blue on the nursery wall; that Dylan should sing
"Tangled Up in Blue" on the in-flight stereo, that *On Being Blue*

should be open on my lap with a postcard of Miró's
Blue II to mark my place; that after six years
your great light should be going out
with you not even halfway done, that I should doubt
and again doubt my little light and dissolve in tears

in taxis, on autumn streets, in front of mirrors;
that upstairs in the attic, a new life should have gotten started,
that I should sit and listen to its soft breath on the intercom
with Dick and Betty, brokenhearted,
pouring wine and making plans; that I should find a home,

after six years, there on West 11th Street
in the very house that you and Isabel both had to leave
for Barcelona, London, so that you could live
and work and breathe, that I should leave it for the blue and
      white
of my flat and sit and try to fly a kite

of words, try to keep it straight
as the outflung arm of the David you sketched to make a
      point,
the sling still in his hand; that you should not paint
and paint, your strength still with you, and your sight,
your arm outflung to the starry night.

BATHTIMES

"Meeting of the waters": curious natural phenomenon caused by the meeting of different coloured waters of two rivers which run side by side without getting mixed.

—Tourist brochure, Manaus

I meant to push the boat out, Murphy,
sometime around the start,
not of our voyage but its third year—
to hoist full sail on oūr little brig
and make for the open sea,
to quit my quarters
in the stern, in the stew,
and stop behaving like an Admiralty prig;
throw overboard the spoilt governess,
the pressed man, raving, the mutinous crew;
take the helm and steer us
by all the stars
to a place of fewer storms than calms . . .

But you threw out bathwater-baby-Captain Bligh
and left me to sink or swim,
paddling my pirogue
at "the meeting of the waters"—
one black, one rust-brown; left me high and dry
to frig and frot myself, toss and turn
and fret and fume
and watch a watermark, a stain,
descend the bathroom wall
like the coastline of Brazil
on an old chart dotted with palms,
watch the pebbles, shells, dried seaweed
slip under grimy dust and disappear.

Have I gone to seed? Have I, my arse . . .
It's just that, adrift
with my harpoon gun
and native charms
I could go a week or more
without hearing word from anyone—
only the groan and creak
of timbers, the protesting shriek
of gulls, and when I might think
I was set to go ashore
to surf and flowers and yells, the sift
of black and rust-brown sands in an hourglass
that looks like a twisted heart.

SOMEONE'S LIFE

In a sentence or two
from someone's Life
of someone else
who has become you,
you carry plastic bags
with yogurt, cutlets, peas,
bread, ham and cheese
to your mother's house
which was once your house,
past windows in backs
of houses that were never yours,
windows, walls, doors
which open on lives
that were never yours;
lives no one tells
(there is no one to tell),
lives one could not hope,
in chapter after chapter,
in a single life, to capture:
in which, any moment,
someone will lift
an oval of Pears soap
from the scallop shell
where it slithers in its glop
as, once, the scallop,
and feel in his palm
the child's glass oval
he would agitate
to watch a blizzard drift
and swirl and settle
round manger, shepherds, kings—
then holding out his arm
and tilting it slowly
he sees them, glowing

in that richly tinted globe,
caught in the amber
of a suburban twilight,
of a late-Edwardian summer
that like the Empire
went on and on forever
through Sundays without number
of fish paste and cucumber:
grandfather and grandmother
pouring tea like a river
in Africa or India
as hot sun pouring
through the bathroom skylight
glints on the tea things
and George V, Queen Mary
and a cluster of aunts and uncles
look on sternly, glaring
from their ovals
of burnished metal . . .
He will take scissors, talc
from a crowded shelf,
dry and dress himself
and go downstairs
to the sound of talk
from a sitting room
at the door of which
he stops and stares:
at row on row
of burnished frames
propped on the piano,
at women's floppy hats
and shapeless dresses,
girls' amazing tresses,
flannel bags and spats;
the talk has stopped,
nobody is there
and he does not know

whose life this is from—
this dust-filled air,
these faint smells
of lavender and cat's-piss,
these sofas, chairs,
these wedding pictures,
watercolors, this
grandfather clock,
its one hand stopped,
this rabbit gun
with the broken stock;
someone's, not yours,
not his, but theirs,
all this, nobody's Life
that no one tells—
husband and wife
for forty years,
the husband dead and gone,
the wife living on
with cats for company;
shuffling, she appears
in the kitchen door
and you set down
plastic bags, take out
from your bountiful store
bread, ham and cheese,
yogurt, cutlets, peas
and say, to this
helpless, frightened woman
who was once your life,
whose life now is you,
"Mother, sit down.
Here is your cup of tea,
there the supper I will make
in a sentence or two."

AUBADE

Birdcall loud at five;
the slap of rain
against the grey windowpane,
the slow drip of being alive.

A goods train judders
to an anguished halt,
the pipes digest their fault,
the cat yawns and shudders.

And quickening fear
beats in my chest—
I reach for your shoulder, breast
but you are not here.

FROM
THE DRIFT

CHOPSTICKS

She struggles with her chopsticks, and I watch her slyly
as she mounts a two-pronged attack on a mound
of noodles, or pincer-prods a shriveled prawn around
its dish of gloop. I watch her as she shyly
sets down the chopsticks and picks up a spoon.
Chicken and cashews, sweet-and-sour pork; no shredded
    beef—
It's too difficult, what with my teeth—
and special fried rice. Dinner will be over soon,

ten years to the night since he died, and I concentrate
on fashioning from my chopsticks a mast
like the masts on the model clipper ships he built
and rebuilt and rebuilt and rebuilt
hour after hour, night after night, working late
threading cotton through the tiny balsa blocks—a stickler for
    detail—
to make the rigging shipshape on the imagined past
into which, in his little room, he'd set sail . . .

Someone's singing, *So merry Christmas, and a happy New*
    Year
and I tap out the beat with my chopsticks; *Is everything all*
    right?
You're very quiet. Everything's fine, Mother, let me sip my beer
and remember how we sat with him—ten years to the night—
how we sat with him till it was nearly dawn
and watched him try to breathe,
the white bed between us, and him on it, and grief
no easier now there's a tablecloth, a plate with one sad prawn;

remember how I sat at the piano with my sister
to play our duet—"Chopsticks"—over and over, ad nauseam,
killing time until he came in to pour himself a scotch
and start Christmas day. The clipper ships
still have pride of place in the sitting room, the museum
where I'll sit for a "nightcap" among his prints and pipes,
and pour myself another scotch from his decanter, and watch
the late film while my mother dozes and my sister,

miles away, plays "Chopsticks," for all I know;
where I'll sit and think of ten years gone and her two cats
    gone,
gone with the Christmas dinners, my grandmother and great-
    aunt,
with the endless Sunday mornings, Billy Cotton on the radio
and the endless Sunday lunches of roast beef,
gone with half her mind and all her teeth;
she watches me as I place my chopsticks together. *Go on,
finish up that last prawn.* But I can't.

INHERITANCE

Herringbone and fern, this coat
materialized on the grouse moor,
on ground my self-made great-grandfather treads
ten years before the First World War,
shotgun cartridges, tobacco shreds
and dry flies in the pocket of his coat,

and the slender hip flask,
silver in its leather sleeve,
tarnished now from trying to relieve
my grandfather's thirst, take off his fear
of rats and snipers and the feeble cheer
that goes up as they go over. Last-nip flask.

On the way to art school dances
or a Left Book Club lecture (Spain)
my father glances at his gold-plated watch
and slips the flask, half-full of scotch,
back in the pocket of his coat. At Alamein
it stops a shrapnel shard as he advances

and he comes home, when the war is ended,
to a place where quiet lives are led
(grandfather, father both long dead,
grouse moor and money all long gone);
a wife and kids are all he gambles on
but some things, like the fence, are never mended.

And he gives me, not yet twenty,
the flask, that I will later lose,
the coat and watch, that I will wear and use
to seem a man in the world I have not fought for,
worked for, even spared much thought for.
This is my inheritance. It is plenty.

ANCIENT HISTORY

Kids now don't know anything about history. History is Daddy.
And Daddy is history. —Joseph Brodsky

Your leaner, younger face, your leather coat—
but for the raked beret, the darker hair
and thirty years, it could be me,
out with a girl, out to impress,
unmannerly, unthinking. The pubs I took them to ...
That was the time I learnt about the "real you,"
the weekend life you led aboard your boat,
your evening pub life, gallant, hail-and-well-met
in the Admiral, the Viceroy or the Empress,
favorite of barmaids, at ease among your peers—
jokes followed jokes, doubles followed beers.
At twenty-five, your gaze is challenging, uncertain, self-aware;
your fist clasps a giant enamel army-issue mug of tea
as if it were a pint of Courage. Dutch courage, maybe.

*

"Dutch courage," you called the stoneware bottle of Bols
you brought back from a business trip and stored
in the rich-smelling dark of the sideboard.
It lasted years. A cut-glass, diminutive glass
or two at Christmas, a sip to reward yourself
for mowing the grass or putting up a shelf.
(I came across a painting by a Dutchman, de Bray,
In Praise of Herring, your other little treat.)
And Holland was the Hook, or else Breda,
home to Paul and Els, survivors of the family
who'd shared with you their cellar, rations, fear ...
They moved on, artists, conventionally free,
you lost touch. To cover your retreat you joined alcohol's
Dads' Army, dug in for the duration, drank it neat.

*

Neat in its ranks, my Airfix model air force
endlessly prepared to scramble, my miniature shock troops
overran the house. I hefted your old tin helmet
and charged a pillbox in the garden, or
sniped at the grinning Toby jugs above the pelmet
from my foxhole in the wrecked back room. My war
was loud, bloodthirsty, and a farce,
Hollywood or Pinewood, war-comic stuff. And yours?
I had no way of knowing, and you never spoke
about the names and faces of your six lost years,
your campaigns, North Africa, Sicily, France;
what made you cry out in the night. Was it choice or chance
that brought you us—me, my sister's pop groups,
our mother's moans—your disappointing peace?

*

"Peace and quiet" was what you said you wanted
when, demobbed, you married the unhappy girl next door
and settled down to make a living by your pen-
and-ink. Well, that didn't work, though peace
and quiet was what you got, and a Box-Brownie camera
for recording holidays at Pop's west-country place,
and Pop's boat to potter on, until
he and it and everything slid down the pan.
("Pop" was my mother's father, portly, RNVR,
the planter-sailor-schoolmaster of her girlish passion.)
That's all ancient history. You seemed not to hear her pleas
to find a better job, but went on being haunted
by those sunsets on the Hamble, and used your skill
on drawings that were always just behind the fashion.

*

The fashion that year in birthday cards
had changed from the Impressionists
to Japanese prints—the "Fond regards"
that used to come accompanied by *Mists
at Westminster* or *La Serveuse de bière*
now came with *Cranes* of the Edo period, Rimpa school
or (I still have this one) Naganabo's *Owl*

in Moonlight. I was thinking of you looking lost
among the rows of Hokusai's *Great Wave* and wondering
if I had gone too far beyond your ken—
a student wearing prewar motley, flowing hair—
for Ryecroft R.A.'s *Tall Ships Racing,* when,
my eye drawn up a shingle beach by cables, runners,
I read "With love" in *Boats on a Kentish Coast.*

*

"Kentish Coast" was on the posters at the station
when we set out for day trips—Folkestone, Dover, Deal—
our "summer holidays." The ferry horn farted, loud
and clear through salt-rich air; the deck-chair crowd
sat resolutely frowning out to sea,
preserving their McGill-inspired integrity;
rock pools, weak sunshine, towels stiff with sand,
transistors, thermos flasks. I shivered as I held your hand
and splashed in the shallows, or watched your powerful crawl
until you stopped and, treading water, slick as a seal,
gazed at the grey horizon, the slopping sprawl
that twenty years before you'd plunged into
from a landing craft, weighed down by rifle, backpack: you,
who'd thought the icy heave might be your last sensation.

*

Sensationally alive, weathered, fit and well,
hands in the pockets of your anorak,
in Falmouth, on a slipway—dinghies and a ketch—
you frown against the glare and think of getting back
for a mackerel supper, then the Ship and Bell
where you will stay long after closing time to sketch
old salts in skippers' caps, and big-bummed girls,
all jeans and yachting sweaters, lips and curls . . .
The snap falls from a book of Bentley's cartoon types—
startled aunts, blond hostesses, black-tie diplomats—
and I am crying for the innocence, the charm
of this thirties, fifties world, shopping baskets, bowler hats:
your world, yet not—who once, in beret, shorts, two stripes,
frowned at the glare and leant on an Egyptian palm.

110

GALATEA

"When you left, and I was thinner-skinned
and thinner than I've been for twenty years,
I sat there in that little beach café, half-drowned,

the smells of vinegar and steam all round—
and that was probably what started up the tears
that wouldn't stop outside, my eyes stinging in the wind . . ."

Then, half a lifetime later, I woke up here,
dawn mist lifting on the seafront, the shut-down pier,
bench-dotted gardens and the shingle shelves

where we lay like sea creatures on the seabed,
blind, antennae groping, soft and slow
and wavering as weeds; the click-click in my head

was the sound of pebbles falling over themselves
in the hiss and sigh of foam when it withdraws,
of her high heels on the pavement when we walked together

to the pub, the station, through the worst of weather
and I was left to scrunch through broken bottles, claws,
bleached brittle crusts of starfish, crab, an oil-blackened bird,

a salt-rich tide of little deaths—and I heard
again the liquid clicking I had come to know
as the bubble that welled up in her hot center,

that rose from the seabed, burst and reformed
under her busy fingers, before she let me enter.
The generator throbbed, tugs and dredgers swarmed . . .

Would I find her, shorter-haired, twice-married,
crying as she used to when she lay awake
and listened to a squat colossus, watched it rake

our bedroom with its cyclops eye? No, she is spindrift, carried
on the wind, the voice of one ill wind or another
that blows me and my leaking boat no good—

Whenever you go out, in your little craft of wood,
your little craft of words, it will be me you hear,
it will be me reminding you of how you scorned your mother

and all women who loved you (God knows why),
it will be me reminding you that you will die,
it will be me reminding you of everything you fear.

FÜR ELISE

On her answering machine, Beethoven's *petite phrase*
I heard a hundred times a day when I was eight or nine
and my sister, five years older, practising for her exam.
She took her grades so seriously each night brought a
    migraine;
sometimes she'd stop and shake with fury after just three bars
if she wasn't perfect. And now I wish that I'd learnt too
(I refused the lessons, the piano was *hers*, like the phone)
since even listening can show me for the fraud I am,
a "music lover" who can't read a note and barely
    understands
the structure of the simplest piece, like this one—let alone
the later string quartets; or how unhappiness and pain
are made safe and beautiful, far from what I knew
then and can't handle now—unsmiling silence, my mother's
    sign
of disappointment; the aching head in shaking hands.

BRIGHTON RETURN

A few days off for some fool conference,
and now you drag your hangover round what remains
of the place you wasted five of your best years in—
getting stoned on grass, going out and getting beers in
and getting up to start again at three
and getting off in bed-sits, and not getting AIDS—
recalling last night's "think tank," and the nonsense
talked by G——, and how everyone seemed sober
except for you. The pale sun of late October
warms the stuccoed crescents, redbrick lanes,
shutters of Refreshment Rooms, boarded-up arcades,

and you remember how it was you found each other
in this past its best, out of season seaside town:
South London boys both mad to make your mark,
as hungry, fierce and hampered as the shark
in the seafront aquarium, twitching for the sea.
You shared its rooming houses and its thousand pubs;
to you he was the chosen one, the brother
you'd never had, and you grew inseparable here,
among the smells of salt, wet rot, stale beer,
walking into wind and fine rain that would drown
the words you threw away like twice-smoked stubs.

Now he's dead, you scan the all-absolving waters
as, once, you watched a speck far out, beyond the pier,
grow larger, more like him each time it rose and dipped
(always so far removed, so clenched and clipped)
when he swam back in towards you, waiting: he,
so like and unlike you—why should he have drawn
the short straw? Why should he—a wife, a son, two
        daughters . . .
while you . . . Gull cries and a sudden rasp

of chains, your own life slipping from your grasp—
at the Mini Golf you watch a golf ball disappear
into the gulf below your feet, below the little lawn,

and shiver. Go on, past the wrought-iron terraces
of the prom, the storm-lashed, ocean-liner blocks,
blistered beach huts, silent funfair, Family World's
deserted paddling pool—to the place that claimed your
      girl's
unhappiness and yours: a "clifftop eyrie"—
a bay window, a patched and paper-peeling double room
where the gas fire sighed all winter at your carelessness,
the kitchen where you stirred hot drinks to nurse
her colds, her aches and pains, her "curse";
past the wind-battered, sea-blue-painted box
(Lifeguard, First Aid) to the cliff walk, "The Coombe,"

that sandy, scrubby, gorse-dotted bit of ground
where you got her to agree the thing had died
and she ran off in the rain to cry. Rigging whines
and rattles in the yacht marina where you wrote those lines,
"through wood and weeds, washed up" (alliteratively)
"like bottles, torn shoes and a plastic cup, we walked
      without
a word, and parted"; a giant claw dug up the drowned,
gouged up the seafloor gravel, and you'd wake
with plaster in your hair, survivors of an earthquake,
or wet and raw, sea creatures on a slab—she cried
to see those too. Back now, to the gulls' angry shout,

the littered beach, the breakwaters' ancient calluses;
last light on the grimy swell, the scum-topped surf.
Mast lines clink in moorings that a salt wind scours.
Remember how you used to stand for hours,
hunched deep in your collar, staring out to sea?
The flag with "Lifeguard" flaps, a swirling tidal wash
slaps the pier's once pearl-white, rusting palaces;
slate-grey breakers chase the foam-tossed shingle
up the shore. Forty, scalding-eyed and single,
you turn back to the town that was your "turf."
What now? Refreshments? First Aid? Hours of tosh?

ALBATROSS

Do you still live in your little boat in the sky?
she asked, who once lay and listened to the wind and rain
lash the beech outside, listened to it creak and strain
like a full-rigged schooner; listened to "Albatross"
by Fleetwood Mac and played along on air guitar . . .
And I do, I do. Seagulls wheel by my windows
or hang bobbing on their strings just long enough
for me to look into their baby faces (should I wear
a seagull, hung round my neck?); crows flap across
the Westway to their crow's nest, or gather in the bare
beech tops, huge X-rayed lungs, to watch me die,
it seems to me, while I smoke and wait for what comes,
or pottering after breakfast, playing "Albatross," throw them
    crumbs
that the wind takes: crumbs of comfort, not comfort enough.

FOUND AMONG
HIS PAPERS

And so, all hope of glory gone for good
Like mist that fades before the sun's first heat,
I turned back to Manaus, to the trade in wood,
The preparation of a ghostly fleet.

A year, two years; and now I had to see
Again, before I died, the teeming port
That held a long-enduring lure for me,
Where, among the boats tied up athwart,

I'd first gazed at the long thin stripe of green,
Immeasurably far, the other side,
And at the swift pirogues that plied between;
Where, assailed by beauty, grinning, brown-eyed,

By sacks of manioc, slab-sided fish,
The reek of spices and the open sewer,
I'd first caught the sickness of the English
And feared both its embodiment and cure.

Companions gone, and all contentment gone,
Desire, the cinder of itself, burnt out
(A taste of ashes where it briefly shone)
And each wide purpose shriveled to a doubt,

Did I truly think then, in the hour of need,
That I would find once more within my reach
The simple, secret and essential seed—
Kew, Malaya, I, and everybody rich?

Could I have known, the first time I went home,
High priest and agent of the scientist's creed,
That in the hold, in trunks of tropic loam
Grew one man's ruin, and another's greed?

I saw the far-off ground of our devotions,
And grove on grove, and villages untreed,
I saw the rubber barons and the oceans
Of white blood those groves would ooze and bleed.

And I saw how we had planted desolation;
How on dark river faces I would read
The death of hope and of each trading station,
The rotting wharves, the jetties choked with weed.

I loitered on the quayside, haunted bars,
I let the days fall through my useless hands
Dead as dead matter dumped among the stars,
Sweated through nights in dreams of other lands,

Other lives—my own life a kind of dream:
I woke to what I felt I'd never known,
Voices, names, the black and sluggish stream
All lived by, horizons lush and overblown.

But not me. When I'd drunk my fill of rum
And poured it out again, red-eyed, in tears
And told my sniveling tale of how I'd come
This far, from home to hell, and bent the ears

Of the tenth unlucky trader in a week,
And left behind his disbelieving leer
And stumbled into stifling darkness for a leak,
I'd drag my feet down to the harbor, hear

The quiet slap of water round the piles
And look long at the still, black, wrinkled sheet
Of moonlit estuary—beyond, the isles
Too distant for my searching eyes, too sweet

The clear enchantment that I tried to catch
With gulps of deep-drawn breath, salt breath.
Back to the oil lamp and the sputtering match,
I called it death-in-life and life-in-death

STREET LIFE

I come home at all hours; all hours she receives
her callers, her gentlemen friends, upstairs.
In the street, a car draws up, she breaks into a foolish little
    run.
I know her. Even in the rawest weather, she wears
no tights or stockings, leaves three buttons of her blouse
    undone.
Seeing me, calling, she comes over. We are alike, we share
the same sad, comical fear of being caught
together on our corner, of our long views falling
short, of being caught, of being caught.
Flirting with me, she fiddles with her hair, her shoes,
makes something up when I ask her how she got the bruise
that cascades down her cheek, the purples, reds and blues
of a fruit tart; the colors, almost, of my glans the night
I paid her twenty quid and pushed it up her, dry and tight.

THE SHORT STRAW

You were telling me again how Heinrich Schliemann
had discovered Troy, and George Grote, who was *the* man
in England, was blown out of the water—we were scrambling
     up
the hill above Knossos, you were so far ahead
your voice drifted back to me from the bottom of a well, the
     well
"into which a courtier of Minos might have dipped his cup,"

and suddenly I was alone with the vast blue silence
of the sky and the Aegean and the blaze between two islands,
with the green flames of cypresses and the white bull in its
     cave;
there among the other black-eyed, straight-nosed girls who
     stare
forever into the future from their wall, was Annie's grave
Minoan face, her mouth opening to tell me you were dead . . .

Too late. Too late for us to patch up our quarrel,
for me to award you the palm and you to give me the laurel
as we sit to ouzo and retsina and a huge heaped plate of meat
that is nameless, that you, having set to, name and eat
in a back-street taverna, the owner calling out
Why aren't you eating my liver, and you, *As Prometheus said*

to the vulture; too late to laugh at our falling-out
over little cakes and honey in Ammonia Square,
to settle our differences in the garden of the British School
where you showed me Byron's letter and Evans's chair;
too late to recall our laughing fits, the cackle and drool
of the old crone who served us *horta* every night, and our
     dread

of her snaggletoothed fixed grin, and the shits and squits
that were, you insisted, her revenge—she was one of the
        Furies,
one of the Erinys, and we had been found by all the juries
of all the gods and heroes, guilty of the crime of contempt;
too late to tell you of the different fate I dreamt
for you: the Eumenides appeared at your deathbed

and they were kind, they treated you kindly, they called off
the white coats and the black suits and finally they hauled off
the great bird that had its beak and talons in your entrails,
so you got up and went home and, since you were forty-one,
the age at which Schliemann gave up the day job "and all it
        entails"
and set sail for Asia Minor, you let yourself be led

by your nose for the salt-sown fields, for the smell
of the wine-dark seas off Crete and the meat smell of
        Heraklion,
the whiff of burning charcoal and the resin smell of wine
poured from a plump wooden cask, you picked up the thread
and followed it back into the labyrinth, past the steaming pits;
the Minotaur had been killed, and you were well, you felt fine.

                        *

The day I heard, a day like any other, was for you
one of the days that you had left, one of the few.
Annie told me. She thought I might want to write
and I did, I meant to, to make up for years without a word—
but instead I went back to the out-of-season seaside town
that chose us, and it hadn't changed, it hadn't heard:

the terrace-crowded hills that fanned out to meet my train,
the salt wind and the fine insistent rain
had not changed, nor the fairground bulbs that put the *bright*
in Brighton, nor the Grand, the Metropole, the squares
of rust-streaked stuccoed houses, market streets, sea airs;
and the bookie and the resting actor hadn't heard

of the glamour and the pain of being us, how we'd gone down
to rotting B&Bs, the redbrick box that was our birthright,
the library steps that lifted us above our station;
two bookworms who dressed older than our years,
who had no time for the time-pissing politics of our peers,
striking poses over coffee in the common room's mass
    exhalation

of Gitanes smoke; how you stood your ground
on the "obvious superiority" of Graves to Pound,
Steely Dan to the Stones, Empson to anyone "meretricious,"
    "trite"
or, worse, "unmetrical." When you went back to Loeb and
    Ee-*sky*-lus,
eschewing villanelles for good, I tried not to take it
    personally—
husband-to-be, you had to defend the fortress you had made

(the dinner things washed up, the breakfast table laid)
against the armies of the mad, wife beaters, druggies, drunks;
    against
the fans of Che, the friends of Chile, the iron-fisted, iron-
    gloved
of Czechoslovakia; against my playing part-time anchorite
when I wasn't playing part-time *poète maudit* . . .
Now it's been breached, and the wise moderation that kept
    you tensed,

and was so hard-won, looks like the kind of sick joke I once
    loved—
Beckettian, Hitchcockian—I once found so much to my taste
but haven't now the stomach for, and *A stupid waste*
is all I can think, confused, contrite
and queasy as if we'd been on the beer. But it's you who are
    so sick
your stomach's almost gone, on whom time has played this
    trick,

mindless, meaningless; and when I heard you'd said, half Waugh,
half Stoic, "I seem to have drawn the short straw,"
I felt all your bravery and all your fright,
the years dissolved, I was that same night owl, that same
    night-hawk,
I saw you put a cigarette to pursed, fastidious lips, set down
    the stylus
on "Katy Lied," or slam outside to walk and walk.

*

As I did, when I heard, I went back down
to walk the beach, to talk it all away, or clear my head—
but I couldn't put my finger on the flaw,
I couldn't see why you should have drawn the short straw
and I should still be here, picking up the thread
and reeling in the years, breathing salt-rich air;

however many times I muttered to myself *It isn't fair*
no one would come to make it all all right.
How could you, who sat up quietly reasoning all night
to make sense of the mess of Maggie's and Joanna's lives,
leave me with these loose ends, unreasonable, a rack of knives
honed by memory, that cut me whenever I go near them?

So many things to ask, though you can't hear them—
How did you shake off the demon muses that we served
and live well? Did I get more of everything than I deserved,
while you got less? Did we outgrow those boys who stood at
    a slant
to the universe, who drawled *The more things happen to you,
    the more you can't
tell or remember even what they were*—an inseparable,
    insufferable pair?

Now it's pointless, why do I remember how we'd wail, "I—
I wish I could swim" with Bowie going full tilt, and dismay all
    comers
with our paraplegic-robot dance? Remember two long summers

of taking papers to the beach and watching with one eye
as the language students peeled off jeans and T-shirts, and our
    despair
at the sight of beautiful, Parisienne Brigitte, and the way

I fell in love so easily and wanted to be led astray?
Pindar and *Phèdre,* regular meters and irregular verbs?
And "popping next door" to the pub, and our *confrères*
and *soeurs,* George and Kate and Ian and Nicole, and all the
    beers,
and all of us dancing to "Dance away the heartache, dance
    away the tears"
and my "fundamentally irresponsible attitude to herbs"?

Remember the laurel in our tiny yard, and our cat stalking
    there?
Christ, won't you answer me, or look up and frown?
You can't, for fuck's sake, I'm still talking to myself,
talking as I slog through the salt wind and rain
to The Railway Bell, a quick five, then back on the train
where I see you, suddenly, jump up to the bookshelf

and with one of your great asthmatic gulps of breath
take down your precious pre-Socratics, saying *Death
is nothing, dying all; it must not be allowed to scare
old men or girls. In every street and square, behind the rows
of rusting balconies, our lives are being lived by those
who will never know us, or know we lived, and will not care.*
                    *
Which leaves me precisely where? In the lurch,
at a loss, in tears in Great Malvern's Priory church
for all the times you diffidently starred,
time out of mind: the times you made a meal
out of making dinner and served up a blistered, charred
and ruined rump of something or other, and intoned,
        "Behold,

126

a burnt offering to the household gods"; the times you told
that joke—once, in a dingy Athens hotel room with a bottle
of Metaxas and "the best view of the Acropolis by night"
and we watched it all appear in hazy morning light,
by which time you had conveyed the essence of Aristotle
and the all-important break with Plato; and the times, surreal

but oh-so-real, I took it into my poor head to drown,
my poor drink-maddened head, and I went down
to the shore and flopped into the surf, and you fished me out;
the time I taught you the use of rod and line and reel
and you caught everything in that stream, you even caught a
        trout;
the time on a sweat- and smoke-filled night train through
        France

you expounded Descartes, in a nicotine and coffee trance,
to a carriage full of soldier boys (*"Esprit,"*
you said, *"esprit* and *corps* are quite distinct, you see?"*);
the time you let rip at the top of Devil's Dyke,
Andra moi ennepe . . . to a few sheep and a solitary shrike
and, as you went on, Homer's lines exerted their appeal;

the time you gently but firmly showed the door
to that barking-mad, blood-caked, gate-crashing bore,
or showed a clean pair of heels—though one of them, your
        "Achilles heel,"
was thick with bandages—to us, the tribe of Keith,
as we shambled up the hill towards Blackheath
one Sunday lunchtime; the times I discoursed on the void

according to Sartre and Camus, and summoned Proust and
        Freud
as witness to the depth and darkness of our self-deceptions
and called on Swift and Celan, Oedipus and Lear

to speak the unspeakable, the brass tacks of our raw deal;
and you countered with Epicurus, *What is there to fear?*
and insisted that *Call no man happy* must admit exceptions,

that rather than be stymied by the tragic sense of life
we must look to the future, we must find a wife
and let love be our guide and not the words of long-dead men;
the times I this, the times you that . . . *Those times*
are gone, and if you now console yourself by making rhymes
I'm glad for you; sorry for the hurts you strive to heal.

*

But I am gone too, and your words can't make me live again.
You made the pilgrimage to the place where we were young—
"South London boys both mad to make our mark,
as hungry, fierce and hampered as the shark
in the seafront aquarium"—not bad. Isn't this
a bit much, though, so far from the usual vinegar and piss,

some might think you were overdoing it? Aren't I a hiccup,
a hiatus in the line of heroes you set out to elegize?
I wasn't famous like some of your other friends,
the scribblers and the chatterers who, when one of them dies,
line up to write the obit and deliver the memorial address.
I worked hard, loved the life that I was lent and died unsung,

a provincial schoolmaster, far outside the latest trends,
the fads and fashions in the supplements, the Sunday press
such as became your life. I gave up drink and clung
to order, to the middle way, the balanced view;
it was clear to both of us we were on different paths, it's true,
at sixes and sevens, and the harm went unrepaired.

But you must know all things change, and all things stay the
    same:
that's not the wisdom of the ashram, far-fetched, far-flung
hippy-trippy stuff. Or sophistry. The self I mastered—

prince of the common room, of the pub when I was
        plastered—
is clay; I am my loved ones' memories, a name . . .
My genes live on, my mind, in yours and younger heads, as
        well.

And your spirit, so lofty and hilarious, so highly strung?
I thought you judged me. I was sure you could pick up
the acrid reek of my pretensions and self-love, the stench
of affectation I gave off whenever I despaired—
those lines I was always quoting, "Why, this is hell,
nor am I out of it," and more besides, more esoteric,
        French . . .

I thought you a blind fool for leaving Annie, yes,
and I didn't share your épater les bourgeois *taste*
in art and literature, your nostalgie de la boue, *your fierce*
attachment to the weird and arcane, to extremes, to excess;
I didn't trust the charlatans you plunged headfirst among,
I didn't think thrash-rock the music of the spheres.

But I absolve you of all that, and abjure you not to waste
whatever time you may have left. Reeling in the years?
Living in the past, I call it. Look ahead, look higher,
lift up your voice a little and give tongue
in your own words, not Leonard Cohen's; tune your lyre,
pick up the thread, the loose ends. That choir . . .

                        *

And Bach rings out now that you have gone into the ground
and I am going back to my life, my life that is wrong,
that I cannot put right, and we have gone our ways
again. *In ihm leben, weben und sind wir,*
the words I cannot believe, both prayer and praise,
praise endlessly; and all of love is in that sound,

it is farewell and greeting, welcome in a quiet house, rest.
Vergnügte Ruh', beliebte Seelenlust, they all join in song
who did their best and are done with it, those ordinary souls,
our fathers and mothers, and Laura's father and Nicole's—
so thin, so elegantly dressed—and all are smiling, they hear
the music that is all about them, each a special guest

and each just like the others. *Heute wirst du mit mir
im Paradies sein* they sing, and for a moment this is true,
truer than the only world I shared with you:
democracy of lecture halls, of cold damp rooms!
Democracy of dead white males, our pantheon, cold in their
 tombs!
And you are in your grave, and so are Robert Graves

and William Empson, Philip Larkin, Francis Bacon, Sam.
Beckett (as he signed himself that time in my theater
 program),
Tim Buckley, Harry Nilsson, Marvin Gaye; they share the
 earth
and the equal sky with emperors, footsloggers, free men,
 slaves,
with Racine and Callimachus, Velázquez and Vermeer.
Süßer Frieden, stille Ruh'—but I must labor, I must bring to
 birth

this child of grief on memory, and so I think of Bach,
"the most stupendous miracle," his not a moment's doubt
that music was a gift from God; why should we not weep
with somber joy to hear that huge host sing, *Ach,
wäre doch mein Abschied hier, mit Freuden sagt' ich, Welt,
 zu dir:
ich habe genug?* I have enough, I ask no more, devout

and calm of heart, of tranquil mind, like Simeon I see
die Freude jenes Lebens schon—the joy of that other life.
There you sit amid the male-voice choir of almighty heaven,
the chorus of the dead, it is February 1727
and Bach conducts you all in this, his first great work of that
    year;
he is forty-two, the age you did not quite come to be,

the age I am now, though I have neither wife
nor child (*Vergnügte Ruh', stille Ruh'*) and you are dead,
my tears are for myself, since death is but a sleep
and a forgetting; you sing, *In deine Hände befehl ich
meinen Geist,* and instead of forgetting there is music,
there is song, *Have mercy on us, Lord, deliver us from fear.*

THE ROAD LESS TRAVELED

I've never scaled the heights of Macchu Picchu with a
    backpack
or trekked through India, breakfasting on hunger,
or listened in the African night to the insects' claptrap,
smoked a peace pipe on Big Sur, or surfed Down Under.

I never featured on the corkboard in your kitchen
among the postcards from the friends who'd gone to Goa,
Guatemala, Guam; among the glossy shots of lichen-
and liana-festooned temples, girls who grin *Aloa!*

I never wrote, "I have walked the sands of Dar es Salaam
and seen elephants drink from the great Zambezi";
"Moving on to Bogotá"; "Babar says *Salaam*
from San Francisco"; "Here in Maui the living's easy."

(I always sent my greetings from a *caffe, camera* or *chambre*
with a view of the Rose Window, Bridge of Sighs,
    Alhambra . . .)

But if I stand on my rooftop in London, West Eleven
with my head in the clouds of Cloudesley Place, North One
I can get it clear: how one day you'll move earth and heaven
to have me here, but I'll have changed tack, I'll be gone

in search of some more fascinating place or person,
I'll have made a fresh start, with no thought, now, of failure,
it won't be my emotions that you play on (or rehearse on),
it won't be my tongue that tastes the coastline of Australia

in the birthmark on your thigh; it won't be me who brings
    you
tea in bed, or a cappuccino with the froth still on it,
or performs my "Dance to Morning" for you, or sings you
"The Shadow of Your Smile," or writes a double sonnet

to you, to your freckled breasts, your sturdy
dancer's legs and neat behind (or, if that's too wordy

for your answering machine, ghazals
to your eyes that are the color of the clear green water
of Sardinia), or puts on *"El cant dels ocells"* by Casals
and holds the phone up to the speaker, or holds your daughter
to the sunrise in a suburban garden with galahs
and kookaburras, holds her up as if I'd caught her
to hear the song of the Catalan birds, and Bala's.

BARCELONA

What was I doing here, haunting the dead?
From his studio in a derelict cigarette factory
the windowless windows of the derelict warehouse opposite
were blind eyes overlooking the ochers and umbers
of his palette—I saw his corduroys and scarf,
his slicked-back hair, his head thrown back to laugh
a nineteenth-century, *La Bohème* laugh. But he was gone
and I sniffed stale air for a word I could use,
a word for his life, his art, for the night he went
to be chosen to die by a thing he did not choose,
did not see . . . It was late, I wanted to go to bed
with his beautiful German widow, but she talked me
into submission and downstairs to the *calle*
where someone was shouting and waving a knife
at a woman, his girlfriend, model, wife . . .
Back on the Rambla there was safety in numbers,
or so I thought. I wanted you. It was your scent
I'd caught, wandering by day around the Gothic quarter
where you had struggled through a "difficult" year
on a language teacher's wage; I'd joined the throng
in the cathedral cloister, stood below its vault
of tattered palms and counted seven fat white geese
that gobble-squabbled under them, for crumbs, for release,
then at my hotel in the little square
I'd sat with chestnut blossom falling in my beer
and imagined it falling in your hair;
when I had to eat, what you ate, what everyone eats
in Barcelona, I'd breathed in every tapas bar
the now-familiar amalgam that you are—
the sweet, the garlicky-pungent and the salt—
and remembered you come dripping from the water
for me to frame in the crook of your freckled arm
our cubist village and its single palm,
our spaghetti-western beach, deserted for a shoot-out

at high noon, when sunlight struck it like a gong.
I'd remembered how I "wore my impatience on my sleeve."
Now I was heading for the waterfront—God's truth—
to drink in its wind-braced, salt-stiffened air
when the Rambla caught me in its wave and bore me on
to a little red-lit, low-lit booth
where I watched two strangers—brisk,
methodical, expressionless—ride out their storm;
slap, slap, he ploughed her salty furrow, warm
and wet and open wide, he gave no thought to risk
as he poured ambergris into her waiting mouth—
and tugging at myself, so raw and dry,
I wanted to believe, in art that doesn't die,
in whatever lives on in a Gothic-baroque-cubist heaven
with sea nymphs riding dolphins, sea creatures, shells,
with clouds and putti, far from these semen smells,
these blade and needle-sharp, blind-eyed streets.

DIARY

I should not have read your diary. Maybe,
I thought you would not have left it open on the floor
if you hadn't wanted me to read those things
you never could have said. But then the words
that spoke so thrillingly about your other lives—
with me not in them, anywhere!—leapt like knives
from your hand, and I knew I'd chosen
my own hurt, and yours. I'd wanted us to be—
not *free bloody birds,* but the galahs with painted wings
on your parasol, heading for the sun; I'd wanted to write
ghazals to your eyes that reminded me of the sea,
not read the endearments you'd entered there, the trite
and tender phrases about him, and not me . . .
But you were rich and strange to me once more,
rich and strange with all the little razor strands
that cut me when I took the diary in my hands.

CRASH

You'd lost your pearls. You told me as we slowed
to single file past churning lights, an ambulance, the rain
reflecting red off tarmac and the shiny backs
of accident POLICE. Everything turned raw—
from our slog towards a sleety last resort
through laurel-crowded suburbs suffering the weather,
to the box without a sea view, the overpriced hotel
(its paneled lounge, school-dinners smell
and *Reader's Digests*, its walks for neither health nor sport),
then this, the stove-in metal and approaching chain saw.
And you had lost your pearls.

They were the snake dance that we did together,
they were the little globes of light that shone
to light my darkness where they fell, where you fell,
backwards on the duvet, plumply pillowed. They were all
you took with you when you made tracks
to here, your little something for a rainy day,
a present from your mother, part of who you were,
her daughter, far from home—*and what were they to her,*
a single row of Japanese pearls, what were they to her,
the chambermaid who found them? You stopped to make
    a call
from the next service area and looked like death
warmed up by neon and we both knew they were gone.

The tailback cleared, you swung into the fast lane
and put your foot down to the floor and kept it there,
the car held on, held its track towards the white
pearl strings and necklaces of London, you held on tight,
tight-mouthed the whole way back while I held my
    breath . . .
I could see you, naked but for your pearls, a cliché

I still tasted, I could remember making you a small
gift of pearls that glittered on your breast, your chin
then melted off. I glimpsed them in the windscreen
as the bright rain hit it and was swiped away.

FÜR ELISE (2)

Tu parles joual? From high above the grey St. Lawrence,
the early settlers' houses were a stage set, out of scale.
The fields of Abraham. The field of battle. We'd made peace
abruptly in the hotel lift one night, after three days
of sparring over lunch and dinner, speaking looks
in the special papers and the plenary sessions, unspoken stuff
joking with the late-night crowd in the St. Lawrence bar.
The kernel of the hard core, I called her, Elise, young star
of Montreal, Quebec City; I could see through the tough
and witty surface, see into the pale grey eyes and the books
of poems for what she wanted me to see, or so the pale gaze
seemed to tell me; I knew the craving for release
that a single mother like her must . . . I couldn't fail.
Tu vas jouir? Three months of phone calls. Letters. Torrents.

(*Joual*: A form of popular French spoken in Quebec province and par-
ticularly in Montreal. Though attacked as ungrammatical, phonetically
corrupt and full of Anglicisms, it has been adopted by many Québecois
writers since the 1960s.)

SALT

The morning after, the morning of the memorial affair
for Michael V., Michael "mine's a treble bourbon
and [a line of] coke" Vermuelen, I walked shakily into
    Hangover Square
and a voice in my ear whispered, "Are you still that suburban
boy who dreamed of taking opium with Baudelaire

or wine with Byron, of setting sail from Greenwich to Durban
with Sir Francis Chichester? Will you never learn—
that some mistakes are final, that the heart gives out,
gives up, that you should expect the unexpected turn
of events that leaves you all at sea, that whoever lives out

of a hip flask and a coke spoon has it coming to him, or to her?
You've been in the wind and rain of your inner weather
for so long, you've barely noticed what's been going on.
The world has dumbed down, the century is almost gone.
I'd say it was time you got your shit together.

Remember summer evenings when that smell came off the
    reach,
greenish wood at waterline, froth that factories had spilt,
dead gulls, dead fish, tidal leavings, pungent silt—
remember treasure twitchers on the pram-wheel-littered
    beach,
the words you cannot outgrow: *trade routes, Trafalgar,*

circumnavigation; do you think the tides will bring a glimpse
of the fabulous, of the man's life, sunk to the hilt
in your place and nation, you might have led if not for your
    vulgar
wish to make it with these middlemen, the pushers, pimps
of literature? I may be smiling as I always was, but look
    twice—

I knew what everyone was worth, I knew your price
and what each of you had or hadn't failed to make
of your enormous luck. Everything I did was its own
    double take.
Some nights I'd work till dawn to make my Guyville yours
and I was king and you did my bidding and I opened
    doors.

Who would have thought I might exhaust the vast store of
    me?
(The bottles and the lines lined up. I dispatched them with
    contempt.)
All the signs were there, but none of you ever dreamt . . ."
Later that same day (for I have drawn a veil
of hot tears and old malt and songs that never fail

across the afternoon, and night was falling fast)
I saw a plaque on both the houses I was swaying past—
the one belonged to Francis Chichester,
the other to Frédéric Chopin. I whistled a Chopin
    nocturne
and suddenly I was all business in the stern

of *Gypsy Moth IV;* on board were Brad Leithauser, dressed
in the sailor suit he wore in *Querelle de Brest,*
and an old salt, made of sterner stuff; but where
were Chichester—Sir Francis—and Frédéric Chopin?
Where were they now, when I needed them most?

When I'd mislaid the next bar, and that lighthouse was a
    lamppost?
And where were Christopher and Edward, *mes copains?*
Suddenly the same voice was serenading me:
"You will never achieve an expression of love for the sea
like the *chansons* of Chausson, or hear what song the sirens

sang to Claude Debussy; you will never find yourself in irons
with Conrad. Your verse bobs like a little yacht
in heavy seas, dismasted, it veers and bobs and weaves
as if it were the *Galatea* at the mercy of great waves,
as if the helmsman were unfit, a soak, a sot

who didn't know his perihelion from his periplum
or periplus, his pabulum from opium or rum."
When, I thought, when had I been blown off course?
For there they were on my starboard beam,
two white ladies on the rocks, a blessing and a curse.

There came faintly to my ears a snatch
of that old Dylan number, "You can be in my dream
if I can be in your dream," and I'd picked up a dose, natch,
from a pickup in the last port of call—
which might have been Portobello or Porthcawl,

it hardly mattered—a market street, a narrow strait
where I used to jib and tack and navigate
between the packing crates, remnants of commercial passion
and the hulks becalmed in a Sargasso of yesterday's news,
yesterday's rotting fruit and veg, their loafing crews

cupping hands round steaming mugs and yawning,
where I would come about and heave to in the early morning,
put in to some safe haven, drink my coffee ration
and remember how I went upstairs with Margery or Kate—
it hardly mattered now that I was drifting, out of drinking
    water,

past a coast of jagged rocks and pines (O *my daughter*)
and it could have been a wharf in Soho or Shad Thames
that loomed out of the fog, pale outstretched hands
groping for the gunwale, clutching stems
of glasses or belaying pins, pens, brushes, swollen glands,

I heard the gentle slaps of water as it rocked the hull
and the voice of some dead master, mariner,
both one and many, friend and foe, in the cry of a gull
that came through the "small hushed waves' repeated fresh
      collapse,"
I knew the face that bobbed before me in the updraft

and beckoned me towards the cockpit, but when I went aft
the deck had disappeared, I stood in shit-clouded shallows
and the bird flapped and flew around my head: "Aloes.
A little something for the weekend. Ambre Solaire.
Jojoba. Such were the unguents that you'd apply

to salve each other's arms and legs and backs
when you'd burnt them. *Life's a beach, and then you die—*
Remember that? How mad for the sun you were?
And all the trains in which you made impoverished tracks
through France to the Italian riviera, *mare*

mediterraneo? You were on a pilgrimage, to Rapallo's
boulevards where Pound had strolled, to Sestri
that surprised you with the Via Byron and his old
palazzo on the 'Bay of Silence,' and Livorno where
they plucked out Shelley's heart and burned the rest—

'the darkness he embraced was nurse not bride,'
that line you both loved . . . Remember the violence
of your last coming together, and what you later wrote,
that stuff about the cyclops in the new marina
and your Galatea, your *sunt lacrimae* note,

all salt and water, half-remembered myth:
'we walked without a word, and parted'? My arse.
Scenes, tears, a year of learning your three Rs—
remorse, regret, recrimination—that's what it took,
and afterwards you put the whole lot in a book

and told the world how much you loved her, but it was a
    lie . . .
Half the time you are your own worst enemy
and now you're back to taste her seaweed and salt
and ask yourself if it was all your fault
as you've done a thousand times; or do you hope to have her
    sea anemone

for the price of a double at the Grand? Have you no shame?
Put it behind you, as you have your jottings from
the boudoir of some provincial Don Juan, and refrain
from opening old wounds, scratching at old sores.
These rocks and breakwaters, this pebble beach, this prom

lashed by the English waves, the English rain,
will always call you back—what metaphors
could better anchor you to the permanence of loss?
Love and work, the imperatives I leave you with—
I, your conscience and your albatross—

are all you have. You've grasped you're no more immortal
    than
your friends, than any mother's son, any mortal man;
so cast off your moorings, take the helm
and steer your own course until you can be free,
attached and free. Deep water need not overwhelm

or threaten you. Your end is life. Put out to sea."

PATIENCE

If I think of my grandmother's house, I think of these:
the black lacquered cabinet of curiosities
that held a Buddha and his temple, intricately carved
in ivory that was yellowing like old teeth, like the keys

when I lifted the lid of the polished black upright
piano that no one ever played, that made a soft, blurred,
tuneless noise, half-felt; of the diminishing black herd
of elephants that patiently crossed the mantelpiece

towards the water hole on the wall to their right,
and how, as they trooped and bellowed, trooped and calved,
all that was left of the real herd after forty years,
they bore witness to the skill of ivory-workers . . .

Nelly the elephant, I sang, aged four, close to tears,
packed her trunk and said good-bye to the circus;
off she went with a trumpety-trump, trump-
trump trump, yelling along to the wireless as I pedaled

my tricycle furiously round the floor
under the eye of the black, beribboned and bemedaled
grandfather clock, between the legs of the green baize
table on which my grandmother laid out cards for patience,

running the gauntlet of frowning vague relations
faster and faster, round and round, one eye on the door
but tied it seemed to the settee, prickly old frump,
the trembling, tintinnabulating nest of trays.

Was it the boldness of her move that drove me on
and the thought of her all alone that made me want to cry?
For forty years I have been trying to say good-bye
but I did not want them to leave me, and I have not gone.

MALAYA

In Bayswater, where she came to live
to save her mother's life, she forgot Malaya,
the rubber trees, the heat and the veranda,
her amah, and her brother's ayah.

To save her life, she forgot: Malaya
and her mother slowly wasting, fading
in the slow wet heat. Her brother's ayah
saw a white blur on the darkness, saw

their mother slowly wasting, fading
in St. Mary's Paddington, attended
by King George V, Queen Mary; a blur, then darkness; saw
her father at the bedside, tight-lipped, sobbing.

In St. Mary's Paddington, attended
by the angels and ministers of mercy, her mother
saw her father at the bedside, tight-lipped, sobbing,
though she did not watch. Her mother died—

angels and ministers of mercy, her mother—
when she was ten years too young
to know that as her mother died
half of her father died also.

When she was ten years too young,
too young for fear, for emptiness,
the other half of her father died also,
his heart breaking on the garden path.

Too young for fear, for emptiness
that called to her as she wheeled a pram—
her heart breaking—on the garden path,
she saw the life that started in her baby son,

who called to her as she wheeled his pram,
called to her from his cot. At last
she saw the life that started in her baby son,
the life she'd live, since nothing else was left.

Called to her from my cot, at last
I found myself, after forty years—
the life she'd lived, and nothing else was left—
walking away from her, towards her too.

I found myself, after forty years,
in Bayswater, where I'd come to live;
walking away from her, towards her two
homes, the ice rink, the heat and the veranda.

HOUSE-CLEARING

Her clothes are going into big black plastic sacks
which I tie up, for charity; she no longer needs them,
they are things that have not fitted her for years.
And this *Life* of Cary Grant, these paperbacks
I brought her—*The Penguin Book of Cats, Too Deep for
    Tears*—
they must go as well, she no longer reads them
and I'd say, judging from the dust they've gathered,
hasn't done in years; nor, though she blah'd and blathered

with the neighbors endlessly about my books,
has she opened *those* since—when? since she was moved to
    tears
by how *unhappy* all my poems made me sound?
For here they are, as dusty as the others, and as useless.
And when did she last refer to *Married Love in Later Years?*
Towards the end they slept in single beds, and looks,
hard looks, were all that passed between them, drowned
in scotch and disappointment. Now she's toothless

and the legs that, as a girl, she was famous for
have started to give her hell, and she must leave her house
which we both call home, as in "Are you coming home
for Christmas?," and I can't believe her house
holds so much of her: her clothes in cupboards; in her drawer
a sheaf of letters, handwritten, tied with ribbon, and a poem
cut from Patience Strong; on her dressing table, lavender
    water,
scented handkerchiefs, heirlooms of an only daughter.

Who dreamt that I would be here, wrapping up her life,
her fifty years in this one place as daughter, mother, wife,
wrapping up the precious china and cut glass
for sale by auction, tying up loose ends?
That I would find these notes from relatives and friends,
fusty, black-edged, "With deepest sympathy,"
these snaps that show her, a cut above, in her convent class,
then the woman of the house, house-proud, holding me?

House-proud! The Hoover sucks up a carpet of dust
from the carpet, her sheets and pillow slips are streaked
and a smell of stale pee hangs about in the hall.
The sideboards and the dinner service and the Toby jugs, all
that they inherited, accumulated, held in trust
for the family "overseas," everything that leaked
quiet desperation, wrongness—the home she built:
it must go, and she must go. What's left is guilt.

UNCOLLECTED
POEMS

EFFECTS

I held her hand that was always scarred
from chopping, slicing, from the knives that lay in wait
in bowls of washing-up, that was raw,
the knuckles reddened, rough from scrubbing hard
at saucepan, frying pan, cup and plate
and giving love the only way she knew,
in each cheap cut of meat, in roast and stew,
old-fashioned food she cooked and we ate;

and I saw that they had taken off her rings,
the rings she'd kept once in her dressing-table drawer
with faded postcards, long-forgotten things—
scent-sprays, tortoiseshell combs, old snaps
from holidays when we were children, one
cloudy-yellow miniature of schnapps
he brought back from abroad—his business done,
was he tempted from his usual double scotch?—
but lately had never been without, as if
she wanted everyone to know she was his wife
only now that he was dead. And her watch?—
classic ladies' model, gold strap—it was gone,
and I'd never known her not to have *that* on,
not in all the years they sat together
watching soaps and game shows I'd disdain
and not when my turn came to cook for her,
chops or chicken portions, English, bland,
familiar flavors she said she preferred
to whatever "funny foreign stuff"
young people seemed to eat these days, she'd heard;
not all the weeks I didn't come, when she sat
night after night and stared unseeing at
the television, at her inner weather,
heaved herself upright, blinked and poured
drink after drink, and gulped and stared—the scotch

that, when he was alive, she wouldn't touch,
that was her way to be with him again;
not later in the "psychiatric" ward,
where she blinked unseeing at the wall, the nurses
(who would steal anything, she said), and dreamt
of when she was a girl, of the time before
I was born, or grew up and learned contempt,
while the TV in the corner blared
to drown some "poor soul's" moans and curses,
and she took her pills and gulped and stared
as the others shuffled round, and drooled, and swore . . .

But now she lay here, a thick rubber band
with her name on it in smudged black ink was all she wore
on the hand I held, a blotched and crinkled hand
whose fingers couldn't clasp mine anymore
or falteringly wave, or fumble at my sleeve—
the last words she had said were *Please don't leave*
but of course I left; now I was back, though she
could not know that, or turn her face to see
a nurse bring the little bag of her effects to me.

THREE-PIECE SUITE

The battered leather sofa that spilled horsehair,
that I knocked the stuffing out of, a stiff coarse hair
like wires—my crippled tank, B-17 or Lanc
limping home on a wing and a prayer;

the bamboo table where, in a previous life, she'd taken
tea in the whitewashed, sepia-tinted shade,
that now, Sunday teatimes, was visibly shaken
by whatever cake she'd made;

the painted screen that shielded, once, her mother's bed,
that showed all the richness that had been Malaya's,
hummingbirds, Japonica, a rubber tree,
the loss of which had left a small persistent ache . . .

Her clutching one or other of the three
in the middle of cleaning, wincing, murmuring "My *head* . . . ,"
her singing, *Bali Ha'i, I hear you calling*
from the depths . . . Come to me, come to me;

her defeated air, her telling me to take
from the round tobacco-scented tin of fifty Players
two bright white cigarettes—no filter tips—
to tip the coalman, Jeffries—no first names—

who waited at the back door with his empty sacks
and his rich, mysterious smell, his bright white grin
as he mimed putting a cigarette to his lips;
her grandmother falling, falling

in the night, and the blood, and no one
ever speaking of it, and the grim determination
with which I delivered "coal"—my father's paperbacks—
and waited for it all to go up in flames.

They were married in the winter of '47,
a bad one but for her who wilted in the heat
a blessing, frost-starred. The year of *South Pacific,*
of "Some Enchanted Evening," "Bali Ha'i" . . .

Ten years of rationed happiness. The Christmas '54
end-of-term concert at her father's school in Devon
she sang the aria from *Madame Butterfly;*
curled pink pupa that would soon start to make her sick,

I slept through it; my sister sat with the score
in her gingham lap, jaw dropping as our mother twirled
a rice-paper parasol and hit the highest note . . .
Later, Mummy's little man, I trailed after her

lugging her father's huge ex-navy coat
on my skinny shoulders, I was the busman, I shouted "Fares"
while she heaped up coals to warm their three
unheated rooms, their three-piece suite—

I was rewarded by indulgent grown-up laughter,
loose change chinking, "One please";
as she swept a duster over tables, flicked at chairs
she sang *Some enchanted evening, you may see a stranger*

or *"Un bel di vedremo"* (just the tune)
and dreamt of evenings on the South Pacific or the China seas,
or remembered times she'd partnered him in the skating pairs
but found the noise and crowds too much,

or was a girl in that other world,
rubber trees, the sudden rustle of monsoon . . .
But when had she met the man who stood in our door,
who spoke American to her, who wore

a trench coat that made him look like Gregory Peck
or was it Tyrone Power, who came in "for a cup of tea"
and stayed for hours, talking softly, who moved to touch
her hand? All the years she was at the "beck

and call" of that same granny dear
who would so easily bring her to her knees,
growing madder, meaner, dog-in-the-manger,
and I never thought of how her head swam, how it swirled

on Richmond Hill, not from vertigo for once but to see come
        clear
those blade-etched frost shapes on the ice rink,
whorls and stars, her head always teetering on the brink;
or of how a life could go, could shrivel-shrink

to one overheated room, a stained armchair,
a cheap transistor and a handful of tapes, among them
no *Madame Butterfly* or *South Pacific,* and a glare
of surprised fear when I reminded her she'd sung them.
                    *
It was *Madame Butterfly* as she went into the fire,
it was Maria Callas singing *"Un bel di
vedremo,"* not a dry eye in the house, her eyes
had melted, and all the flesh that had been her,

and the black, bitter growths she'd almost heaved
from her bloated body, all went to ash, to the air
as Callas sang her favorite aria and we grieved
silently, my sister's face crumpling as she hit top C;

her hair that had gone at last to grey, her hair,
her poor bent bones, all went to smoke that curled
from the crematorium chimney—this carefully timed
half hour was all it took; and I thought of how I was free,

of Tyrone Power and Gregory Peck, her father,
mine, and I tried to swallow back the sighs
that shook me, gulps and sighs, and Callas climbed
the scale of grief and longing, higher, higher.

LAUNDERETTE:
HER LAST NIGHTDRESS

A cotton one with a few flowers and a bit of lace
at the neck, her name tag stitched inside, it falls
from my bag of socks and shirts and smalls
and looks so innocent, so out of place
I see her again, hot and flustered in the ward

we took her to, and helpless, late at night
when even she admitted "something wasn't right"
and I left her waving, and she sort of smiled
to say I mustn't worry, must get on,
get back, to sleep, to work, to my important life.

Next day, I went to M&S, I bought
the nightdress she had asked for as an afterthought
and took it in to her, and she put it on
and loved it—no more the sad, unreconciled,
bewildered woman I had fought, no more

my father's tetchy, disappointed wife;
girlish, almost. So it was what she wore
until one day I walked in and found her lying
in a hospital gown, so starched and plain
and straitlaced, with strings that needed tying

while this pretty one had gone into her drawer—
the something that was wrong had made a stain,
a stench I took away with me somehow
to wash, and forgot all about till now
I stand here in the warm soap-smelling air

but can't remember why, and people stare.

THE FIREBREAK

A slow hot firebreak through the burning bush (by Arthur
    Boyd)
and the old tyre up ahead, dead-center of it, dusty-black,
that made a gentle bump as we drove right over it

was a coiled sleeping snake. I shouted *Stop the car. Go back!*
and knelt down and touched the scaly head we'd split,
that was my own two minds for the next few miles;

whatever broken or oozing thing was on *her* mind
she drove in silence and then stopped again, all smiles
and said *Come on, forget it* but I heard the electric hum

of the crickets' disapproval and the kookaburras' laughter
and, high up in the branches of a scribbled-on scribbly gum,
I saw that snake, watching. It opened wide its jaw and hissed

*Either you're suffering from the heat or you've been pissed
once too often, mate. What's got into you? Don't come
the raw prawn with me. A real bloke, having scored a blonde,
would cart her off with him to the outback of beyond,
not write sestinas on her arse. Life is short and death comes
    after.
What are you waiting for? With no children, it's just void.*

And then she started up the car and they were far behind,
the firebreak and the forest, and in the place of fear
there came a new freedom and loneliness. In the clear.

THE OLD STORY

We would meet, as in all such stories,
in the immigrant quarter, near her small hotel.
She had flown in from another country
where her father was dying, her brother in prison.
His passport and papers not in order.
He was shot, of course, ten yards from the border.

She fell in with a family in a big house on the border
between the last uninvaded country
and this place that had lately become a prison—
they all lived on memories of the old order
until she could no longer stand their sentimental stories
and hanged herself in front of the Grand Hotel.

There was an apprentice who worked in the hotel
kitchens, who every day wrote letters full of stories
to his mother and father on their farm in the country.
Sometimes he said he felt as if a border
had been drawn around him, as if he was in prison,
but he knew that everything has an order

if he could only understand it. He took each order
as it came, and sometimes longed for that far country
he'd heard of where the old folk sit to tell their stories—
which are mainly of how life comes to border
on madness, how their children treat the home like a hotel
and what it is like to live in the awful prison

of their bodies. One of them had been in prison
long ago, at a time when every order
had to be obeyed, when it seemed a border
was fixed between right and wrong, like seasons in the country
or the routine in a well-run hotel.
But behind even the most convincing stories

you sometimes hear the note that makes all stories
an interregnum, like a checkpoint on a border
or the lights going out all over an hotel,
a pause, a reversal of the accepted order,
the guards and prisoners changing places in a prison,
for example, or a new life in a foreign country . . .

And we two? That might still be in order—
to cross the border to a strange new country, our two stories
bound into one, a home neither hotel nor prison.

RIO SONG

I was settled in a likely looking bar
drinking caipirinhas chased by beer
when a soft voice whispered in my ear
No money, no honey.

She was sixteen if she was a day,
she wore a black and shining bustier
her black eyes looked at me as if to say
No money, no honey.

Her thin hand stroked my thigh, my crotch,
my wrist (I'd carefully removed my watch).
She leaned back, ordered double scotch;
No money, no honey.

She drank and told me I should go out back
where on a mattress covered by a sack
she'd take my mind off its one track:
No money, no honey.

She'd ease my body too, she swore
she'd do what I told her to and more
but this was the rule for rich and poor:
No money, no honey.

"My brother deals, my mother begs"
(she stretched out, stroked her naked legs)
"I'm not going to end up with the dregs:
No money, no honey."

The air was heavy with the coming storm,
my shirt was soaked, while she was merely warm
my head was buzzing like an angry swarm—
No money, no honey.

She cupped her breasts, she gestured at the door;
the spirit streamed from every pore;
the samba throbbed, I knew the score
  No money, no honey.

I checked my wallet. Checked my keys.
I thought of you back home, thought of disease.
She was already talking to a Japanese:
  No money, no honey.

NEIGHBOURS

When the rains come in Rwanda in a Tutsi village
and the topsoil's washed away, strange shoots
of fingers, toes, knees and elbows, jawbones,

push up from such wrong, unlikely roots
as have lain there since they were slaughtered—
the cowherd and the teacher and the sawbones

and their women and their children and their neighbours
(for unless you are a hermit in a mountain cavern
or a guru in a temple in the jungle, neighbours

are what you naturally, inevitably have,
to share your sunsets and the fruits of your labours),
all waiting quietly now for when they are watered,

when the rains come, in Rwanda, in a Tutsi village.

THE LOVE OF
UNKNOWN WOMEN

Young women with damp hollows, downy arms,
bare burnished legs—you see them striding
towards their plant-filled offices, riding
bicycles to flatshares after work; lunchtimes, you stare
as secretaries, backpackers tanned from birth
peel off their things and stretch on sun-warmed earth.
A few of them stare back ... As if they'd share
their world of holidays and weekend farms

with you! They step more lightly every year,
a glimpse of neck hair, a scent that lingers, girls
who, swinging bags with shops' names, disappear,
trailing glances, into crowds; each one unfurls
her special beauty like a fragile frond
before your famished eyes. *I am what lies beyond,*
they seem to say, *beyond the mortgage, car and wife—*
I am what you deserve, I am the buried life

you will never live. Are they stretched out drunk on beds
by hands that unhook bras and yank down briefs?
Do they wake with tongues furred, heads
hot and unremembering, and gingerly explore
the places that hurt? Crave water running over them,
cool as their long fingers? Tarkovsky, Schubert, jazz—
it's all the same to them. As are your little griefs.
It isn't fair. If you've not changed, what has?

Is it a kind of shifting, as of sands
along a windy, condom-littered stretch of shore?
In simmering parks, on summer streets
where they would never stop to talk to you, you stare,

you note the curve of eyebrow, cheek and lip,
of other things too. In bars you search left hands
for seals of love, or ownership.
They can smell your old defeats.

From
DEAD WHITE MALE

I.M. J.B., G.E., G.MacB.

Flow of waterlight. Unbroken blue.
I have come back to a place of healing,
a place of waters, in search of something true,

to heal my life, because *I have not right feeling
towards women*—because I have played
so recklessly, and lost, my mind is reeling

and a solitary gekko in a patch of shade
shows me companionship, and what it is
to sit and wait, and what I have made . . .

Farewell to that. Farewell the fond embraces,
farewell the nights in bars, the sunlit walks, the wine
I drank with friends, with Joseph, Gavin, George;

farewell the days I watched light fall on their faces
like a benediction. Peace their portion. Sorrow mine.

*

This was no place of safety, or place I could call home:
infernal joys, joys of the deadened spirit.
I looked for comfort but no comfort came.

I went to where a tree stood like a flame
that flickered in the petrol glare; I learnt to fear it.
This was no place of safety, or place I could call home.

Infernal joys of nighttime, deadened spirit
on my tongue, my tongue hot as a flame
and the insects uttering their prayer. Who would hear it?

I looked for comfort but no comfort came
on the cold dark tundra, permafrost. My deadened spirit
flickered in the glare of its own shame.

Now everyone is dead, all places are the same.
I looked for comfort but no comfort came.

*

Their bodies bloom again from graves in corners.
That sudden writhing—is it maggots, tubers
or, white in moonlight, tangled limbs?

Such trite and terrible visions disturb us . . .
We have come again as mourners
to this funeral, which is ours. The air

tastes of leaf mold, frogs croak our hymns,
there is a steady murmuring of prayer
from the ruined chapel—that low drone . . .

Patience, patience brings peace, I know. I pray
for patience now, I gather up my dead
and lead them to a place of healing

and one by one they are made whole, myself too
made whole again, by patience. I am grief's prey

*

The kind, the loving hearts go into the cold ground,
into the dark; into dust and ash they go,
and we cannot follow them, or know

to what rest they have gone, what silence found.
I open a window and am lifted clean out, over the lake—
a great light, water glint, a single swan

gliding over it, and I am lost among gull cries,
the cries of the heartbroken and the drowned.
Peace to them. They are long gone.

Peace to those who leave the works of hands and ears and
     eyes,
console us, comfort us, Johannes Vermeer. Brahms.
My father in your darkroom, my mother making cake

you have mixed developing fluid, flour, and I
your orphan, I am in it up to my arms.

ACKNOWLEDGMENTS

Some of the poems in this collection have appeared in the following volumes published in Great Britain by Chatto and Windus:

In the Hot-House (1988)

Greenheart (1990)

Harm (1994)

The Drift (2000)